DEFINITION OF A LEADER

HOW TO LEAD OTHERS AND BE TRUE TO YOUR OWN VISION

BRANDON SILER

Table of Contents

CHAPTER ONE

EYES CLOSED: THE VISION

Synopsis: How does a young man of humble beginnings defy the odds and become a leader? It all starts with unexpected greatness, uncommon faith, and unusual determination. In this chapter, Brandon Siler will tell his origin story and describe the blueprint for discovering the greatness inside you.

It all began with a vision.

I vividly remember that day. I was sitting in the breezeway of the Pine Hills housing project, waiting with my eyes closed. The Florida sun beamed down on my face, and I smiled, anticipating this day to be unique. It was a Saturday, and that's every kid's favorite day already! This Saturday would be perfect. The occasion? My dad was coming to pick me up.

Outstanding leadership begins with your eyes closed, not open.

My early years were filled with imperfect days of struggle and survival. Our family didn't grow up in the best of circumstances, with all the pleasures of life. We learned that we had to fight to create a life that someone could enjoy. Some people would call us "poor," but I would say we struggled. Even in difficult times, I considered some places my oasis. I kept my eyes closed because I saw the oasis in my mind.

My dad would pull up and take me to Sanlando Park in just a few minutes. Sanlando basketball court was one of the best places to spend a Saturday. As my eyes closed, I could hear a basketball bouncing, shouting on the crowded court, trash talk, celebration, and victory. Sanlando was where all the real ballers played. As a young athlete, I relished the opportunity to run with the adults. I flashed a quick smirk as I thought about how many points I would score.

The old heads consistently underestimated me. Who cares? It was their loss. I'm about to go wild on these...

"Boy!"

All of a sudden, a voice snapped me out of my vision.

I shook my head and sighed. With my eyes opened or closed, I knew who was speaking. That was my momma. I may have been annoyed with her then, but if you know me, you know that my momma was always my inspiration. With everything she had been through, she was still a woman of principles. She was the strongest person I knew and didn't mind using that strength to keep me in line. My momma played no games! When I messed up or tested the limits of her patience, she would lay down the law to make sure I knew what the consequences felt like. Trust me; I felt every lick I received from those belts. It was necessary. I would like to think she knew the high stakes for someone like me. I was gifted in whatever sport I played. Some people saw me as the young Black hope for the community. Plus, a Black boy growing up in an area without much money and no father often meant a life going nowhere fast.

I grew up knowing my biological father was in the same city as me, but he didn't show up for me as his son. The difference between my momma and him was night and day; she was always there. She was consistently involved and present. She treated me like I should prepare myself for anything. Today, she was trying to prepare me for disappointment.

"Boy, don't you be waiting for your daddy all damn day!"

I gave her a response, "He's coming, Momma!" That's what he told me, at least. I was confident, but I can't lie; I was skeptical. My dad forgot everything: birthdays, special occasions, games, all of it. I found out later in life that he wasn't just absent; he was defiant about it. He didn't feel like he had to show up for me. Even with all that disappointment, I hoped he would come around, no matter what he didn't do. As great as my momma was, I craved an actual father figure to help me, love me, care for me, and tell me, "I am proud to be your dad!" That's why I was out at 7 am, in the hot sun, with my eyes closed, waiting for him to show up. He invited me to join him for a day of my favorite activities. We would hit the park at Sanlando to shoot hoops and go fishing. I couldn't imagine anything better!

As always, he was late. A few minutes late soon turned into thirty minutes, and thirty minutes slowly stretched into an hour. I kept my eyes closed.

This day needed to be perfect, just as I had seen in my vision.

After waiting for an hour, my step dad walked past me. "Hey, Jitterbug, you wanna come up with us?" I paused; something in me told me I should go with him. My step dad wasn't perfect either, but he was the closest thing I had to a father figure. He was trying to get his life together. He had served six years in prison. He wanted to show up as an example for my siblings and I. He would take me to his favorite basketball court, at a park, in Winter Garden. No, it wasn't Sanlando, but it was just as fun. I would bond with his friends and I felt like a son. Today, I couldn't go with him. I had to hold the vision. I had to wait for my dad.

"Naw, I'm good; my dad is coming." He looked up to the sky like he knew something I didn't, nodded, and sped off in his car.

One hour of waiting became two excruciating hours. My eyes weren't closed anymore; they were open. I was looking for any drop of hope in a reality that felt determined to disappoint me. I was searching for a father who ultimately would never show up. Why did he do this? My momma was right! He always let me down, again and again. What should have been a perfect Saturday, became the straw that broke the camel's back. This time, I wasn't sad. I wasn't crying. I was angry.

After sitting in my anger for a while, my step dad's car circled back to the front of the breezeway. He saw me in the same spot I was in when he left me. "Aye, Jitterbug! Hop in. We'll go back to the park!" I opened my eyes and hopped in his car. I decided; I would no longer wait for my dad. I would no longer hope for a change in his behavior. Ironically, I was also no longer excited about fishing. It took 20 years before I could go out on the water and cast out my fishing pole again.

My stepdad didn't come back on his own. As my protector, my momma called him and told him to return. She could tell me the truth and had empathy to care for me.

That day, reality changed me.

For some people, this story is about my father and his failures. "Damn, man, your dad ain't ___" (I'll let you fill in the blank). For others, this story illustrates how important it is for other people to show up for you. The lesson from that Saturday is different for me. Reading this book, you'll begin to understand, I don't see life in the same way that others do. I see the world through a different lens.

I closed my eyes, hoping for something that never came. I realized that life is not about your reality. Life is about the reality you can see and the reality you want to create for yourself. Sitting there in that breezeway, I realized I never wanted to feel like that again. On that day, I learned something about vision, and ultimately, about leadership.

It all began with a vision.

From that disappointing Saturday to the writing of this book, I've lived a life that would make a Hollywood screenwriter jealous. A kid from the projects of Pine Hills grew up to be a star athlete, a national champion in college football, an NFL player, a business owner, a millionaire, and a success. Most importantly, I became a leader worth following.

And it started with a vision.

If you pick up this book, you want to be a great leader. My life story could differ from yours in every way, but you will soon understand why I decided to share my story with you. I wrote this book to inspire people, just like you, to become great at whatever it is you have been created to do. I'm here to tell you something that might surprise you. Start by throwing out all of the conventional wisdom you learned about leadership from school and listening to the fancy gurus. Great leadership starts differently than you think. Most people assume that leadership is something you see in others or model after someone famous. I'm here to destroy all of those misconceptions. Those are fairy tales!

Outstanding leadership begins with your eyes closed, not open.

Before you can study what you see, hear what others say, speak your mind, and plan your goals, you must close your eyes. You need to ask yourself, "What do I see when I close my eyes? Do I see the reality of how I'm struggling to lead at this moment? Do I see the vision of someone else that I'm chasing? Do I see the expectations of someone I admire as a role model? Or do I see something special that only I can do?"

I have built my entire life around pursuing one word: Legacy. From a young age, I knew that I was different and destined for something more. Even without a father around to inspire me and the challenging circumstances that I had to grow up in as a child, I knew that I was supposed to be a leader. A great leader!

If you're okay with being an average leader, this book will frustrate you. I'm not here to give you a cliché blueprint of what I've learned from others. I'm not interested in comforting the "average" in you. I want to shock and motivate your system. You can be significant. The vision you see with your eyes closed and the world that you'll create, that vision requires you to be a great leader.

The vision started with me being uncomfortable in average surroundings. Most people ask me now, "Who were your role models?" I laugh at that question. Growing up, I didn't have many people to be inspired by. Instead of having positive role models to show me what I should do, I used negative role models to remind me what not to do. Most of the time, what I saw in my community disappointed me. I couldn't find many role models who wanted more than the life they were currently living. I decided to watch them and do the opposite of everything they did.

"Man, what grades do you make in school?" I would ask someone whose life was going nowhere. I learned they made C's and D's, so I decided I had to make all A's. I realized some of my friends and classmates consistently stayed in the Detention Hall after school, so I vowed to stay away from that place. I found out that some people in my community spent their lives without goals, jobs, or ambitions. I knew I had to establish a bigger vision for myself than my city. That's where it started for me. What does the old Scripture say? "Without a vision, the people perish." I refused to perish with my surroundings.

All great leaders start with a vision.

Some of you will read my story and say, "He's a born leader," but that's not true; don't believe that lie. As you read my story, there's good news for you. Leadership is not something people are born with. All great leaders are made and developed through life experiences, lessons, adversity, and the ability to adapt and adjust to problems.

Not too long after that Saturday, when my father disappointed me, I closed my eyes again. This time, at ten years old, I decided to dream of a different reality than my current reality. I realized I wanted my life to eventually look different from what I was facing. I don't know what made me do it, but in a moment of maturity, I pulled out a piece of paper and wrote down something that would shape my life. I asked myself this question, "What do I want my life to look like?"

What do I see when I remove the limitations and blinders from my mind? After imagining all the things I could do and could be, I wrote down what my life would look like in one year. It was inspiring and ambitious, but I couldn't stop there. I wanted more. I closed my eyes again. When I opened them, I scribbled what life could look like in five years. It was beautiful. That would have been a success for some people, but I wanted more.

After I wrote down my ten year vision, I still wanted something more. That's when I realized God had given me a gift, limitless imagination. God had granted me an extraordinary view of my life, and I truly believed it. I wrote these one, five and 10 year dreams down on paper. I put them someplace where I could constantly see them. My vision can be summarized in one simple, powerful word: Legacy. I refused to stop until this vision became my real life.

Sadly, most people live their lives without vision. They may see something they like for a fleeting moment, but it fades away when they see the work. They scroll through social media and desire the version of someone else's life, and then they keep scrolling. They love fantasy more than experiencing it for themselves. That's not a vision. Vision is something you will obsess over, something you will sacrifice everything for, something you will die to see accomplished.

Even more disturbing, most leaders need a vision for themselves but lack one. They see the pile of bills, to-do lists, and expectations and refuse to see more than what they have now. They are overwhelmed by reality and claim they don't have time to dream. If that's you, I'm here to wake you up! You can only be a great leader with a clear vision.

Another family member who shaped my life was a man called "Gorilla," my grandad. They named him right. He was a beast with hands of stone. I used to idolize him, but time revealed he was also a broken man needing healing. I remember one day, he bent down and grabbed my hands. Staring at me, he said, "Look at these. Do you know why God gave you these two hands? To put 'em on somebody." That's what he did for a living; he put hands on people in the boxing ring, and he was a beast. That's why I have the words "King Kong" tatted on my forearm.

Eventually, his hard work, training, and vision led him to the highest level of boxing. He shared the ring with, arguably, the greatest boxer of all time, Muhammad Ali. I admire Ali because of his skill in the boxing ring and because he was a world changer outside the ring. Ali saw something others didn't. He created a reality for himself and the world. He changed lives and challenged the status quo. How did he do it? Vision.

He said, "Champions aren't made in the gyms. Champions are made from something they have deep inside them – a desire, a dream, a vision."

Today, I'm living in the reality of the vision I wrote down as a ten-year-old boy. I own seven businesses that I run with the help of great teams because I saw a vision. One of my companies, Legacy Pro Sports, has over 5,000 former NFL players as clients because I saw a problem and created a vision to change it. Most importantly, I took the negative examples I saw in my community and saw a vision, a vision of my family where I was present and healthy for my wife and kids.

You may think this is impossible, but in this book, I'll show you how I did it and how you can do it too.

Before you hear my story, I want to ask you three questions. Ask yourself these questions, then open your eyes. They're the questions I'll keep asking you throughout this book:

1. Do you genuinely believe that you can get there?

This is the most essential part of your leadership equation. I know you "say" you believe you can get "there," but do you "really" believe it? I know many people who could see themselves in a fancy car or a big house, but seeing and believing are worlds apart. What are you going to do about what you believe? Has the vision become an obsession you cannot ignore, no matter how hard you try?

That is what separates regular leaders from great leaders. If you believe, you'll do whatever it takes to get there.

2. Do you have what it takes to get there?

Most leaders have a vision for where they want to go but need more resources to get there. This is the next step after true belief. You have to put in the hard work to determine if you have what it takes to achieve it. Do you know the steps it takes to get there?

I am also speaking about the humility you need to realize that you're not the best at everything. No matter what your vision is, you need help to accomplish it. It would be best if you had the right teams, strategies, and suitable systems to bring your vision to reality. Your attitude must change if you're unwilling to assess and admit what you need.

3. Will you consistently work and do the things you need to do to get there?

Do you have that "dog" in you? This is the question of consistent sacrifice. Are you willing to change your life, adjust your rhythm, and sacrifice other people's pleasures to get what you need? I know many people who would love to live my life, but they need more time to be ready and put in the work required to achieve it. The secret sauce to my leadership has always been "sacrifice."

People always ask me, "What is enough for you? When will you stop after achieving significant sports accomplishments and owning multiple businesses?" I laugh at that question now. I realize they don't see what I see. My vision in my head has turned my life into an obsession to reach those goals. I still want the same thing I wanted when I was ten: Legacy.

Another mantra I live by is tatted on my arm: "Good ain't good when greatness is expected." I won't let disappointments define me. I won't let "average" slow me down. I won't let "good" trap me. I want greatness.

After all these years, I still have my eyes closed. After reading my story, I hope you'll close your eyes with me.

CHAPTER TWO

DEVELOPING DISCIPLINE

Synopsis: Why do some succeed and others fail? Why do talented people live lives below their potential? This reflection will reveal the dangers of possessing greatness without the discipline to match it. In this chapter, Brandon gives homage to his mother and challenges the reader to live beyond, not below, their potential through discipline and determination.

"Aye, Brandon, we're heading out tomorrow. Everybody's going to be there. You're coming, right?"

Whenever my friends invited me to hang out or go to parties, I would always roll my eyes and shake my head. I don't even know why they asked. They knew. And I knew too. "Man... You know, my momma ain't gonna let me go to a party."

As a kid, I never understood it. After a long week of school, every child anticipates the weekend. That is the prime time to rest and have fun after the grueling school week. No more homework and extended classes. No more sports practices and workouts. It's the time for parties, sleepovers, and trips to our favorite hangout spots.

I learned early on that my momma treated me differently than most kid's parents.

As much as I loved my momma, she was strict. I couldn't stand it. Every parent has a different leadership style to guide their kids, motivate them to do what's right, and reach their potential. My momma ruled with an iron fist.

> *"Leadership is easily shaped by what you see in the world..."*

Obedience? That was required. Excellence? That was expected. Parties? You can forget about those.

While most kids in my age group were hanging out and doing what they wanted, I was introduced to something that would ultimately shape my future and my leadership: Discipline.

I was the oldest child in my immediate family and one of the oldest in our extended family. In our household, I had a different responsibility. Yes, I was a three-sport athlete. Yes, I pushed myself to achieve the highest grades in the classroom. On the weekends, I was a part-time babysitter.

Picture this: a 10-year-old kid watching six other kids (my brothers, cousins, and some neighborhood kids) on special occasions. My responsibility was to feed, bathe, clothe, and keep them in line. That's precisely what I did. I had so much placed on me that I was driving before I had a permit. I had to pick up my brothers from school and practices because my momma was busy working and providing; I wouldn't recommend this today. I was forced to do more than the average kid. After a brief bout of resistance, I learned enough about my momma to know I didn't want to face the consequences of her wrath.

Someone recently asked about the discipline I received as a kid. I laughed and told them the truth: "My momma was an ass-whooping machine." I know parenting looks different for many families today, but back then, she used physical discipline to make an impression. The times she applied that discipline were rare and strategic, but when she did, I felt it, and I was not too fond of it. There were moments when I didn't like her, and she was perfectly fine with that. After all, she was there to be my mom, not my best friend.

Without my dad around to raise me as a man, I struggled to connect with my mom and her parenting style. I wanted more freedom and fewer boundaries. Looking back, I understand why she approached me that way. I now realize she wanted more from life and wanted her children to experience that too.

As I said, "we didn't have much money in our house," but because of my momma, I wouldn't call us a "poor" family. Yes, we teetered on the edge of struggle and survival. There were moments when we held our breath to see if the bills would get paid. But that's understandable. She was a single mom raising everyone. My father wasn't around, and my brother's father wasn't there either. All the responsibility fell on her shoulders. She embraced it with a mix of discipline and ambition.

Before we moved to Pine Hills, our whole family grew up in one neighborhood in Daytona: aunties, uncles, and cousins; all on the same street. My momma was the first person in our family to leave Daytona and strive for something different. She wanted to go to Orlando, a big city, and establish a different path for herself and her kids.

Every great leader has the power to influence others. She was convinced about her vision for more. She influenced my cousins, Chucky and Bally, to move to Orlando with her. Even today, our families still get together multiple times a week to eat crabs, play cards, and watch football. My momma's ambition for more established something that changed our family. It changed me too.

This responsibility and her way of aggressively calling me to more, was her type of protection. She believed that I was different. It was like she had this sixth sense that I was special. She knew I was the little Black hope for our community, and she was determined not to let small things ruin enormous potential.

She wanted something different for us. I slowly started to desire something different for myself. She took risks and stepped out of her familiar family surroundings. I wanted to travel the world and see more than my neighborhood. She shaped me. She inspired me. She made me see something that others couldn't.

Great leaders are always able to harness the superpower of belief. My momma believed in my potential before I could see it for myself. Just like a great leader, she refused to let me settle for less than that vision. She sold me on her vision until I could close my eyes and see the vision for myself.

There is this misconception in sports, the greatest athletes are the most talented. I have played sports at the highest level, and I can confidently say that is not true. Even as I was growing up, I understood this. My drive was never based on the assumption that I was the most gifted athlete. Others may have considered me the most athletic or talented, but I knew better. As a young kid, I was a starter on all my basketball and football teams, and I ranked 4th or 5th on the roster. My drive was motivated by being the most disciplined. You may be faster than I am. You may be more athletic than I am. You may have more natural physical abilities. But no one will ever outwork me. No one! I learned, although talent is necessary, discipline can take you places that talent can only dream of seeing.

That is the thing about ambition and discipline. Combined, they are unstoppable. They depend on each other to build the life you want. If you cannot see more for yourself, discipline feels like a hamster wheel; it feels like you are running in place. If you don't have the discipline to put in the work, your ambition is just a fantasy. I learned that one cannot succeed without the other.

After seeing how much my momma believed in me and closing my eyes to see a new vision for myself, the discipline to see the vision turn into reality began to consume me.

I didn't get to party with my friends during school, but I always looked forward to the summer. My cousin AJ and I were close. Both of us were athletes. We spent the summer months together at his dad's house. Part of that time was spent as training partners, shaping our bodies for the next year's sports seasons. As a three-sport athlete, I knew that the offseason was the prime time to build the strength and endurance necessary to get through a grueling year of practices and peak performances. AJ and I made a pact to get our bodies in shape together. Although I made a pact with AJ, I also made a pact with myself.

I had a vision and an obsessive belief that what I saw with my eyes closed would ultimately be accurate in my life. "Good" wasn't good enough for me. I had to be the best! I decided to close my eyes again and picture my competition. I convinced myself that some kid was outworking me somewhere in the world. I imagined him getting up at 6 AM and running the streets of his city. I imagined him working out two or three times a day to whip his body into shape. I imagined him getting obsessed with being the best, and I got mad. No, I am the best!

Vision helped me see a legacy I could create for myself and future generations. Vision also provoked me to make another vision of motivation: a kid working harder than me, trying to take my spot and be the best. To me, that was unacceptable. Decades later, it still is unacceptable.

I made a pact with myself that every time we watched TV that summer, whenever a show went into a commercial, I would do sit-ups and push-ups non stop until the show came back on. AJ would do it with me. We were slowly disciplining ourselves into machines. After the summer, I decided I wanted to hold onto this. After all, there was a kid somewhere in the world working out harder than me, even during the school year.

When AJ came back to visit in the fall, he looked shocked when I dropped down on my stomach to do push-ups during the commercials of our favorite show. "You still doing that? I probably did it for about three days when I got back home, but you're still with that program?"

"Man, yeah," I said during grunts of endless push-ups. You may be faster than I am. You may be more athletic than I am. You may have more natural physical abilities. But no one will ever outwork me. No one. For AJ, it was a program. For me, it was the discipline to leave a legacy.

Discipline is painful. It is the most challenging part of becoming great for most people. Discipline is the one element that separates the good from the great. It's easy to get lost in the mechanics of "How to do it?" This is a question I get almost every week. "Brandon, you're so successful and accomplished. How do you do it?" Discipline is not about "what do I do?" Discipline is about "What do I see for myself?"

At the end of Chapter 1, I asked you a question: "After you close your eyes and see what your life could be in one year, five years, and ten years, do you truly believe that you can get there?" This question wasn't an accident. When I say I believe that I have what it takes to see my vision become a reality, I am obsessed with it. I won't stop until that legacy I saw at ten, becomes a reality for generations after me.

Leadership is easily shaped by what you see in the world or your organization at this very moment. Again, if you haven't done this yet, close your eyes. Write down that vision and discover what motivates you to achieve the vision you see with your eyes closed. It will be different for everyone. For some, their discipline will be mental and emotional. For others, it will be physical or spiritual. Whatever it is, let your vision motivate your discipline.

Reflecting on how my momma inspired me to become more disciplined, I've realized some things about myself and my leadership journey.

I truly believed I was special. What gets a kid up before the sun rises to work out? What keeps me motivated and inspired to do everything that needs to be done? I know who I am, what I'm capable of, and what I want to see. I conversed with AJ recently, and we laughed about my workout regimen. He told me, "You were committed to that program. After about a week of being back home, I fizzled out, but you knew what you needed to do." AJ and others saw this in me, that drive to go after it with all my energy and effort. It's odd to think about now, but I believed in the power of self-affirmation.

When I closed my eyes, I saw the vision of what my legacy would be. I put that sheet of paper where I could constantly see it. A day wouldn't go by without me glancing at the list of self-affirmations:

"I'm going to be the greatest athlete."
"I'm going to make straight A's."
"I'm going to have something to leave behind for my kids."

The second I was tempted to slack off or take a step back, I only needed to glance at the sheet. That was my north star for my future and the fuel for my discipline.

CHAPTER THREE

BRINGING THE
BEST OUT OF OTHERS

Synopsis: The test of every great leader is leading others and bringing the best out of them. But what happens when the ones you are supposed to be leading end up teaching you? In this chapter, Brandon tells the story of his brother, Devante, and learning how to adjust when people are unexpected.

I am an athlete. Even to this day, that swagger exudes from me in every room I enter. From a young age, I shaped my life to align with that reality. It could be said that our family was a sports-oriented one, but not everyone had the same approach to life. For instance, I recall the day I realized my brother, Devante, was not cut out for athletics.

I had just come home from school, fresh off a sports practice, as usual. I was always engaged in multiple activities: football, basketball, baseball, track, tennis—you name it, I played it. Beyond sports, I remained active in academics and performance. Not many people know this, but I was actually the lead thespian in the drama department. Acting allowed me to portray reality in a different light from what people saw in everyday life. I also took on responsibilities in student government and other leadership roles. I was constantly occupied.

That particular day stands out vividly in my memory. It was the moment when I recognized Devante had a different disposition. Although we spent countless hours together, we sometimes felt like complete opposites.

As I entered the house, I found Devante lounging on the couch in his baseball uniform, sans cap, socks, or shoes. I was perplexed. You might not realize how peculiar this was, but his baseball game was scheduled for 6 pm. I had hurried home to ensure I wouldn't miss a single moment of it. Yet there he was, nonchalant, sitting on the couch at 6:15 pm. "Dude, what are you doing?"

If you know my mom, you know she's always running late. It's become a running joke in our family that she'd even be late for her own funeral! I had experienced her tardiness on multiple occasions, leaving me in a state of panic. However, with Devante, there was no sense of urgency.

If it were me, there was no way I would be running this late without already being dressed. I would have had everything prepared and been halfway out the door. My mom knew my brother's tendencies. If I were in his position, I would have been a teary mess when we were running late.

"Hey Tae, don't you have a game today?" I exclaimed, rushing through the front door. "Yeah, I'm waiting for Ma," Devante calmly replied, his attention never straying from the cartoon he was watching. I stormed into my mother's room. "Ma, Tae's game has already started. How can you both be this late?" With a smirk on her face, my mom sauntered past me in the hallway and called out to Devante, "Come on, boy." She left the house with no sense of urgency. That smirk conveyed volumes to me. It was at that moment I realized, she and Devante were on the same wavelength. I was the one with the misunderstanding!

They understood that Devante was playing baseball simply because it was what we all did. I was passionately committed to sports as a means of advancing myself. In contrast, he was just going through the motions. He had no interest in forging a long-term relationship with the game. I confirmed this later when I observed his team's head coach giving instructions. He went through every player, assigning positions for the game. "Mario, First Base... Tim, you're in Center Field." All ten kids on the team received positions except for Devante.

I was livid. Who was this coach who thought he could single out my little brother like that? I paced back and forth, struggling to control my anger. All the other kids were deemed capable of playing, but my brother wasn't going to get a chance? Hell no! Just as I was about to storm off the bleachers and confront the coach, I looked into the dugout and saw Devante. He wasn't upset in the least. A broad smile graced his face. He turned around, grabbed a bag of sunflower seeds, and took a seat on the bench. He was content because this was his dream scenario—he had the best seat in the house with no responsibilities on the field.

At that moment, I realized that my mom and Devante were in agreement. My brother had no interest in playing sports. How had I missed this? In my mind, sports were everything and the only thing. Who are you if you aren't participating in sports?

I felt awful for him. How many times had I forced him to do something he had never wanted to do in the first place? How many years had he lived unfulfilled because he felt compelled to fit in with everyone else? That was the day I took a step back and truly considered him. I launched a campaign to convince my mom to stop signing him up for sports. Surprisingly, there was no resistance from either of them. They were completely satisfied with that change in perspective.

Devante, however, possessed a brilliant intellect despite not being involved in sports. From a young age, it was evident that he had a remarkable ability to quickly memorize and process vast amounts of information. One of our main debates revolved around who was smarter—him or me. Devante attended FSU for his undergraduate studies and obtained his Law Degree from Boston University. He still contends that his credentials surpass my undergraduate degree from UF, an MBA, and a Ph.D. Well, whatever... There was always something about his demeanor that convinced me he would succeed in whatever path he chose. Devante's biological father had a different genetic makeup from mine.

As a Siler, all my siblings excelled in sports. My younger brother David and my sisters Lexi and Breonna played college sports with skill and success. My sister Amiya pursued a successful modeling career, which is its own form of competition. My cousin Lewbo played college football, and all my uncles were athletes as well. Even my father received a tryout with the San Francisco 49ers. As I mentioned earlier, my grandfather was a professional boxer. Sports were deeply ingrained in the Siler family's DNA.

However, the siblings on my mom's side had different fathers, meaning we came from distinct genetic backgrounds. Among the four of us in the household, only my two youngest siblings, Jada and Jermalne, shared the same father. Nevertheless, there is a 17-year gap between my baby sister, Jada, and me. To most of my siblings, I served as a father figure and a role model they could look up to whenever needed.

Back then, my mom tirelessly worked to provide for us. As I mentioned before, she often left me in charge when she was away. I would find myself taking care of my younger siblings, and they relied on me for guidance as they grew up. None relied on me more than Devante. As his older brother, I naturally gravitated towards him, offering protection because I always sensed he was different from most of our family members. I watched over him, guided him, led him, and essentially raised him. We were close. I'm not sure when the thought first crossed my mind, but I remember pondering the idea that my brother might be gay.

I developed a strong bond with my stepfather through sports, fun, and shared knowledge. I needed a father figure in my life. Those long days spent playing ball on Winter Garden's basketball courts and our conversations during car rides home meant the world to me. We could discuss anything and usually connected over our shared interest in sports. While my stepfather and I formed a tight bond and grew close quickly, he had no relationship with my brother. If I could see that Devante was different, surely my stepfather could recognize it too. He was determined to shame Devante into changing who he was.

"Leadership is a voyage of expansion and challenge. "

I vividly remember the painful moments when my stepfather would use derogatory slurs against my brother, telling him to "man up," and criticizing his walk and manner of speech. Devante was just a kid, and my stepfather publicly and privately humiliated him. This only complicated my relationship with my brother further. Yes, I wanted to protect and guide him, but how could he accept guidance when he feared hearing the truth from me?

Devante learned so much from me. His brilliance allowed him to take a simple piece of advice I offered and apply it to his specific circumstances. I even taught him the fundamentals—the things any father should teach his son about survival and empathy. I encouraged him to envision his future and seize every opportunity to achieve his goals. We had a great rapport and enjoyed each other's company. If only my stepfather had embraced him. It's humbling to reflect on it now. I forged a connection and found common ground with this man, yet he and my brother remained disconnected.

Gradually, I noticed a change in Devante. I can't say I appreciated the environment we found ourselves in, but he desired to escape it even more. He was determined to distance himself as much as possible from our community. While I always yearned to leave the projects, Devante held an even deeper disdain for our surroundings. I suppose growing up in a home where a stepfather fails to embrace your lifestyle or love you unconditionally creates a rift between you and the people you hold dearest.

As time went on and we remained close, Devante came to visit. My life had taken an upward trajectory, and I was enjoying success in the public eye. He stayed at our house for a week, and it felt like old times. We sat in my "mancave," shared drinks, laughter, played games, and watched TV. I missed my brother. Our shared childhood memories felt distant, no longer at the forefront of my mind. Here we were, successful Black men from the projects of Pine Hills, Florida, and life was good.

About a month later, my mom called me from her visit with Devante at Law School. She said, "Guess what? Devante just told me he is gay." I remember that moment vividly because I experienced mixed emotions.

On one hand, I felt happy for him. It must have been agonizing for him to hide that part of himself from us for so long. On the other hand, he chose to confide in my mom first, instead of me. Perhaps that sounds self-centered, but Devante had just spent the entire Thanksgiving break at our home in Orlando. We spent days together in my "mancave", engaging in deep conversations about everything under the sun. Less than a month later, my mom visits him at Boston University Law School, and he tells her? Why didn't he share this with me when we were in the "mancave"? He should have known that I fully accepted him as a man, as my brother, as family. After all, he wasn't the first gay member in our family—we had many family members who made that choice, and we embraced each and every one of them.

When my brother took that brave step to disclose his sexuality, I learned a great deal about myself and my approach to leadership. Devante's coming-out story is not ultimately about leadership or me. Nevertheless, it made me realize certain things about how I guided him as a father figure. One of the strengths I relied on as a young man was my ability to influence people with my larger-than-life personality. If you've spent time around me, you know it can be overwhelming at times. If you haven't had that experience, you'll get to know me better in the upcoming chapters, trust me.

As someone with a bold personality, I am vocal and opinionated. If I believe in something, I will debate with you until the cows come home. I genuinely enjoy that back-and-forth. Strong personalities thrive in those significant moments. However, what I didn't anticipate was how others interpreted my strength. They saw it and understood it differently. Some viewed my enthusiasm as intimidating.

Reflecting on my years of leading my siblings, I realized that my experiences with them challenged me to become a better leader. I received a crash course in different learning styles and emotional engagement required for effective leadership.

Devante needed to perceive me as a safe space for affirmation, the same affirmations I recited to myself daily. He needed to hear those affirmations from me. He needed to trust me as his brother, as someone who wouldn't pass judgment on him, regardless of his choices. I was forceful and opinionated, and he feared that I might be someone who would judge him instead of a brother who would love him. He knew me as his protector. He recognized the same qualities that made me an excellent leader on the football field, and he found them intimidating when seeking support.

When Devante shared his truth, I learned how to adapt my leadership style.

This realization evolved after running multiple successful businesses. Let me state it clearly: not everyone can handle your default leadership style. In leadership classes, they often discuss various "styles of leadership." Some adopt an authoritarian style, while others embrace a democratic approach. When people ask me what type of leader I am, I reply, "Whatever the situation calls for!" The best kind of leader you can be, in a rapidly evolving world, is a versatile leader.

You cannot rely solely on being a rigid, overbearing leader all the time. That may work temporarily but won't prove effective in the long run. It might bring you short-term benefits but could damage you in the grand scheme of things. To achieve success, you need versatility in your leadership style, the ability to consider other opinions, and an understanding that different situations call for different leadership approaches. With this mindset, you increase your likelihood of attaining the level of success you envision.

This concept may unsettle and challenge you, but it should also offer solace. There is more to you than you realize.

My journey with my brother, Devante, taught me that not everyone will embrace your default leadership style. However, as a leader, you must learn to open the doors of your organization wider than your default style. Some individuals need to be at the table, hearing words of affirmation, while others require a firm direction from a decisive leader. Some, like my brother, fear what you might say or how you may judge them. In such moments, it is your responsibility as a leader to recognize these dynamics and adapt swiftly.

Leadership is a voyage of expansion and challenge. You must ask yourself: "How do I come across to the people around me? Am I willing to change? Am I willing to grow? Am I open to expanding myself and reaping the benefits of welcoming those who may not fully understand me yet?" Years later, I now realize that Devante taught me a lesson about embracing others in my leadership style. It's a lesson I am still perfecting, and one that every great leader must master.

CHAPTER FOUR

BEHIND EVERY GREAT MAN

Synopsis: The most important person in Brandon's life is his wife, Pam. In this chapter, he shares how impactful she has been in grounding him with truth and wisdom. He also speaks candidly about his spiritual journey and struggles.

Behind every great man... you already know the end of the quote. Unfortunately, the statement does not do justice to reality. As leaders, we often fail to realize just how much the right partner means to the realization of our vision. The media tends to romanticize relationships, but the truth is relationships require much more work than what most people are willing to invest. When I initially envisioned my extraordinary goals, I only saw myself. The idea of having a family, let alone a healthy and thriving one, seemed unimaginable. Then I met Pam. We were just kids back then, and yet something about her captivated me. Little did I know that she would become the most important person in my life. While I could achieve great things on my own, with Pam by my side, I could change the world.

I first met Pam in middle school, when my athletic prowess made me the popular guy on campus. The moment I laid eyes on her, I knew I had to get to know her. She wasn't like anyone else; she blew me away. Fortunately, I already had a connection to her through her brother, Tyrell, who was a grade ahead of me. Tyrell and I had a great relationship; it felt like we were brothers. Whenever I spotted Pam talking to her "boyfriend," I would approach Tyrell with a big smile and exclaim, "What's up, brother-in-law?" We would share a laugh, and Pam would get visibly upset. She would tell Tyrell to stop entertaining me, but I didn't care. I was ready to compete for her attention and win her over.

My goal was to always stay on Pam's mind, no matter whom I dated or spent time with. I was determined to never let her slip away. As we grew older, I made sure to stay in her vicinity. I would walk up to her while she held her boyfriend's hand, grab her other hand, and quickly retreat, leaving her flustered. Her boyfriend didn't like it, but there was nothing he could do. I was the star athlete with a reputation for my physical ability. He remained silent, and I persisted. Some might consider my actions bullying, but when it came to Pam, I was willing to do almost anything to capture her attention.

Pam was the captain of the dance team in high school. She approached everything with unwavering commitment. One day, her boyfriend, who was also the drum major, made the team stand at attention on the scorching track. They stood motionless as I watched from a distance. Sitting in the bed of a truck with my friends, I couldn't help myself. I stood up and shouted, "Hey, Pam! Pam! When are you going to leave that chump and get a real man?" Laughter erupted around me, but Pam remained composed, rolling her eyes slightly. Her calm demeanor only deepened my attraction to her. I had behaved like a typical jock, but I didn't care. I was determined to find a way to break through.

We didn't start dating until my senior year of high school. On an ordinary day, I greeted her as usual, and she hugged me. It was more than a friendly embrace; I felt a deeper connection. She was ready, and I wasn't about to let the opportunity slip away.

Pam was voted the most attractive girl in our senior year, but what attracted me the most wasn't just her physical attributes or feminine qualities. It was her unwavering foundation and the strength that anchored her through life's storms. At that point, I observed how her belief system shaped her decisions, and I admired her unwavering devotion.

My relationship with Pam was an unstoppable force colliding with an immovable object. I was the immovable object, refusing to believe in anything related to God. Unlike today, where God is the most important aspect of my life, at that time, I didn't believe in God. This led me down a path of darkness. I had a cynical view of the world and harbored a deep resentment towards anything connected to Christianity and the church. My focus was solely on the tangible things I could see, touch, and experience firsthand. Hard work became my religion, and I dedicated myself to it daily. I observed people in Pine Hills dressing up for church every Sunday, and to me, it seemed like they were deceived into believing in something that wasn't real. When I stepped onto the field, I knew what I believed in: hard work. If I consistently did my pushups while others slacked off, it didn't matter what they believed. Even if they put in the work, it wouldn't compare to my level of dedication. Praying was of no consequence; ultimately, I believed I was better than everyone else.

This mindset influenced every aspect of my life, as I constructed my worldview around the idea that God didn't exist. However, Pam changed everything. She was the unstoppable force in my life, crashing through my hardened exterior. I recognized something was special about her that went beyond physical attraction. She genuinely, wholeheartedly believed in God.

I once heard a preacher say something that resonated with me: "Preach the gospel at all times, and if necessary, use words." Christians are often known for their words, primarily judgmental and angry ones directed at those who don't share their beliefs. This preacher's perspective stood out to me. Our lives should speak volumes about our faith. Can people see evidence of God's work through our actions? Until I met Pam, this had been my only experience of Christianity.

Pam came from a different kind of family than mine. My upbringing was loud, filled with colorful language and boisterous laughter. Our arguments were yelling matches fueled by strong emotions. On the other hand, her family's disagreements were calm and harmless, carried out with intellectual banter and clever insults. I had no category to place this level of interaction; it fascinated me.

Her family was also deeply religious. Attending church on Sundays was non-negotiable for them; it was an integral part of their lives. Religion provided them with a stable foundation. Pam seemed to move at a different pace, grounded in her faith. Her prayers were sincere, and she had a remarkable capacity for forgiveness. When others wronged her, she would be slow to retaliate, often giving them more chances than they deserved. Adversity didn't break her; she leaned on her faith. I had never witnessed such unwavering devotion.

I always believed in my ability to accomplish whatever I set my mind to. However, I hadn't considered the vision I couldn't see. How could I trust the unknown and the unseen? Until then, I had lived fearlessly, tearing through life with reckless abandonment. I was a terrifying mix of aggression and disregard. Restraint was foreign to me, and as a result, I made significant mistakes. Pam's example compelled me to believe in something greater.

Pam stepped into the chaos and recklessness of my world. She planted seeds of what a settled life with a healthy direction could look like.

The transition wasn't easy, as I struggled with my own internal battles.

After thriving in environments where I had control over the outcomes, I began to realize that I didn't have as much control as I thought. Despite my unwavering self-belief, not everyone shared that confidence in me. Despite my outstanding grades and skills, my dream school didn't pursue me as I expected. Other schools overlooked me too. The draft didn't go as planned, even with a stellar college athletic resume. More on that later.

Without a doubt, Pam is the most significant person in my life, as it is through her that God entered my life.

Pam and I worked on my spiritual growth together, from my senior year of high school through my second year in the NFL. The transition to a new version of myself was challenging, but she provided guidance and spiritual structure. The work we did during those years laid the foundation for my spiritual self, which now forms the bedrock of my life today.

My spiritual awakening came at the perfect time, as the next phase of my life would test me to my core.

My pushups theory slowly started to crumble, and it was only going to get worse. How could an SEC Freshman of the Year not automatically gain the respect of his entire team? How could an All-SEC linebacker not be the first linebacker drafted? How could the captain of a national championship team not get drafted on the first day? Even when I did everything right, it seemed like my life was going wrong.

I recounted numerous instances where the rug was pulled from under my feet. Why did God allow me to experience pain when I had worked so hard? Why did my "extra" efforts seem to fail in this environment? Pam consistently showed me that the "extra" element lies in unwavering faith in God. She wasn't just consistent; she was exceptionally consistent. Whenever we argued, Pam turned to her faith, finding the strength to remain level-headed, even when I acted out or when we disagreed. She fought through our battles by leaning on her faith. If she had arguments with family or others, she would engage in prayer, seeking guidance and peace. There are countless attractive women in the world, but how many possess both physical beauty and godly character? Pam had both, and her consistency drew me closer to the light.

This transition didn't come without pain and heartache. Shifting from a life devoid of faith to one centered on God felt impossible. At that point, I wasn't fully on board because I couldn't grasp the concept of faith. Faith meant accepting things beyond my control and understanding. It meant acknowledging that I couldn't handle everything on my own and that I needed to learn the reasons behind certain events. This was unacceptable to me. When bad things happened to good people or when situations didn't go as planned, I expected God to intervene and protect me.

I slowly began to understand that if God did exist, He wasn't a pushover. He wouldn't fulfill our every desire because He knows what's best for us. Sometimes, God plans to enact justice in our lives and discipline us. Growing up, I rarely encountered this aspect of God; had I been exposed to it earlier, maybe I would have had a better understanding. God doesn't allow us to do whatever we want without consequences; forgiveness is part of His character, but so is accountability. God ensures that we receive wake-up calls at the right time.

I also struggled to comprehend why God didn't show up whenever I thought about Him or when I desperately needed Him. Why didn't He reveal Himself to me? Pam helped me see that God is precise, and if we believe in Him, He will show up for us. But if we don't believe, why would He bother revealing Himself?

Pam's patience and unwavering belief in building a relationship with God ultimately caused my life to blossom in ways I never thought possible. But at that point, I was fueled by hatred and couldn't easily turn the corner to trust God.

I believed the church and Christians were fake. I thought praise and worship were manufactured, especially when people failed to live out what they were praising God for. Christians seemed like hypocrites to me. Many churchgoers were judgmental and mean-spirited. Unfortunately, this attitude made those who didn't attend church or engage in religious rituals feel that God loved them less. Overcoming this perception of the church took me years. As a young man seeking authenticity, I had never seen someone genuinely live out their faith and connect it to their life.

Pam was that person. I couldn't resist how drawn I was to her spiritual focus. She was a different kind of woman.

Pam laid the foundation for my leadership journey because through her, I saw the steadfastness required to uplift someone beyond their own limitations. I often resisted her advice and recommendations, at times denying my belief in any of it. But she stayed by my side, gradually chipping away at my heart, not through words but through her actions. She lived out her faith and showed me how it could be done.

Without a doubt, Pam is the most important person in my life because without her, God wouldn't have entered my life. I knew I wanted to be with her, but little did I know how much I needed her to save me from myself.

CHAPTER FIVE

THE GIFT OF BEING UNDERESTIMATED

Synopsis: What separates the Top 1% of all successful people? Is it their wealth, connections, or influence? Or is it their humility to remain a learner despite adversity? In this chapter, Brandon will share his journey of recruiting and navigating the adversity of being underestimated.

"You ain't got 1,000 more Brandon Siler's nowhere."

I will always remember the thrill and rush of being recruited to play college football. If there was a real moment of accomplishment for me, it was receiving that first scholarship offer letter. I finally saw the fruit of my labor. As a boy who grew up in Pine Hills, I hadalways heard that I would be different from everyone else. I was about to play football at the next level. After I received my first recruiting letter, I immediately pulled out a map of the United States. I drew a line right down the middle from West to East. I loved football but was not too fond of the cold weather. The top half of the U.S. was off-limits for me, and the bottom half, with warmer, southern climates, were the only schools in play. I refused to play in cold weather. I had respect for schools like Ohio State and Michigan. Their history was impressive, but I'm a Florida boy to my bones.

My recruitment started picking up around my sophomore year.I had a list of schools I would consider. The school letters were piling up into stacks of paper that felt like mini-mountains in my room. Despite all of this, I knew where I wanted to play football.

Honestly, I never thought I would be a Florida Gator. Growing up watching sports on TV, the only place I wanted to attend and play at was The University of Miami. When they were "The U," they were untouchable. The swagger, the intensity, and the dancing on the field all were infectious. I watched them play in big games and would beam with excitement. That's me right there! I loved how they played, and I dreamed about putting the jersey on. Then, one day, "The U" made that official call. Finally, my dream was coming true.

The Miami Linebacker Coach called my high school coach. I don't know if I've ever been more ready for a conversation! Kennard Lane, another highly touted recruit at Evans High School, had gone to play at The U before me, so our area had already produced Miami football signees. The coach couldn't see me, but I wore full Miami Hurricane gear. At this moment, I felt my football career was about totake off.

Like a kid speaking to one of Santa's elves, I started smiling and talking a mile a minute. "Yeah, coach! I love Miami. It's the best football school! I've always wanted to be a Miami Linebacker." I couldn't believe this was happening. Then, the conversation took a turn. "Okay, well, you ready to commit?" My smile subsided as I glanced at the phone. Why was his tone so cold? Did he not hear that I was a fan? Why did I feel like this excitement was just a one-way street?

I continued, "Uh, coach, I'm only in the 10th Grade. The U will always be my first choice, but I want to keep my options open for now." Silence. After a brief pause, he said, "Well, you need to commit. Look, we got 1,000 more Brandon Silers waiting on this scholarship, so you better hurry up before you lose your spot." After growing up a rabid Miami fan and dreaming of being a Linebacker at The U, I slammed that door shut.

That's when the switch flipped. With a straight face, I said, "You ain't got a thousand more Brandon Siler's nowhere!" and hung up the phone. If you know me, you can assume I said it more colorfully than that. My high school coach looked at me with wide eyes. "There's no way this kid just said this to a coach at Miami." "Forget him," I thought. This coach had no clue what I had been through, what I had faced, or my character. How dare he compare me to other kids he had seen elsewhere! I would prove him wrong and make him eat those words. I threw that matching Miami outfit in the trash as soon as I got home.

It was disorienting to encounter someone who did not believe in me. Of course, I had experienced doubters, some of whom were close to me. They would comment and try to poke holes in my dream, but I brushed that off. However, I wasn't ready for the rejection I would receive from the next level. College rejection was different. The schools that I idolized rejecting me felt shocking, and it wouldn't be the last time I would experience this.

I turned my eyes to Southern California. If Miami was the glamor program in the South, USC fit the bill out West. They had Heisman trophy winners: Reggie Bush,Matt Leinart, bruising running back

Lendale White, and everyone's favorite Coach Pete Carroll. They were flashy, aggressive, and confident, all the things that Miami had with the beautiful L.A. climate. After Miami fumbled the bag, USC quickly skyrocketed to the top of my list.

As my recruitment progressed, USC came to the State of Florida to recruit just three players: Myself, Keith Rivers, and Kenny Ingram. Because we were all in Central Florida, we knew each other well through photoshoots for the media and All-Star games. There was a mutual respect between us. Whenever we saw each other, we would joke and swap dreams of playing together at a school of our choice. Keith and I knew Kenny would ultimately head to Florida State and play there. Any team trying to convince him otherwise was wasting their time.

When you believe that you can change what you're facing and create a different reality for yourself, you can fuel yourself...

Keith and I turned our sights to other schools. We even took a trip to the University of Florida together. Shortly after, I committed to USC, and Keith followed suit. We were the #1 and #2 Linebackers in Florida. I refused to be intimidated by the competition. To that point, I had never thought someone was better than me when we lined up on the field. Plus, Keith was only a linebacker. That was his sole position in high school, making it no surprise that he flourished there.

On the other hand, I played multiple positions on the football field. I could play my familiar role of linebacker and also play running back, receiver, special teams, and anything my team needed. I knew I was the better all-around athlete, so I welcomed him to the Trojans.

Keith, Kenny, and I arranged a visit to USC together. Since we were all from the same area, we wanted to live it up with each other before our lives changed. I received a call from Kenny the week of our visit to USC. "Hey man, USC just called me. They said they couldn't recruit me any further because they have too many Junior College commitments at safety. So they won't even let me go on the visit anymore."

"Damn, I'm sorry to hear that, bro," I replied over the phone. "But we all know you're going to FSU, so... you're good, bro!" About 15 minutes later, my phone rang again. This time it was a call from one of USC's coaches, Lane Kiffin.

"Hey, I hate to tell you this, but we have too many Junior College commits at Linebacker. Therefore, we're not able to recruit you any further." I couldn't believe it. Not only had my dream school turned me down, but now my backup school also rejected me for some Junior College recruits. I immediately called Keith, and he hadn't heard anything from USC. He was the #1 linebacker in the country while I was on the lower end of the Top 10. Reality had set in. They wanted him and not me.

Beyond the rejection and failure, it was the first time I had ever wept in my momma's arms. I remember her saying, "It'll be okay, baby. It'll be okay." I was devastated.

This reaction may sound more dramatic than it should. You're probably thinking, "It's not like you wouldn't receive a scholarship to a major school. You have every reason to be disappointed, but why are you devastated?" Part of my devastation was the unique circumstance that I found myself in. At the time, my recruitment was officially closed. I was fully committed to USC and was not entertaining any other offers. As spots continued to fill up, I was worried I would be stuck in a mid-tier program and not have the chance to make a significant mark in college football. Without national attention, how would I make it into the NFL?

There was a deeper reason why this rejection affected me so profoundly. At that moment, it was hard to explain what this meant to my future. It all goes back to that vision that I had for myself. The vision I closed my eyes to see years ago felt so close yet so far away. My dream depended on getting as far away from Pine Hills as possible. I desperately needed to escape an environment and community I felt would ultimately restrict my dreams.

If you have sat down and charted out a 5, 10, or 20-year vision for your life, you know that it eventually becomes all you can see. Every decision, every significant relational choice, your life is obsessed with bringing your dream into reality. At that moment, rejection felt like it was threatening my ability to realize that vision. That was the moment my ideas turned dark.

Vision requires proper motivation. When you believe that you can change what you're facing and create a different reality for yourself, you can fuel yourself in two different ways. The first way is love. The embrace of others and the positive affirmation you receive from those who care about you can create a burning flame of beautiful love inside you. Then, you can begin to develop healthy pictures of motivation for yourself. Next, you pursue your vision to build the world around you.

There is another way that you can motivate yourself: Hatred. Hatred is the dark side of your motivation. The rejection of others and the negative energy they send your way, their words, and actions of doubt can create a burning flame of anger inside your soul. You begin to create unhealthy pictures of motivation for yourself. You pursue your vision to prove others wrong.

This teenage version of myself leaned heavily into being fueled by hatred. In this season of my life, I was not in a mentally healthy place. My mind was darkening in ways I wouldn't understand until years later. I was unhealed. All the trauma from my younger years was beginning to catch up with me in destructive ways. What started as a drip, soon would become a flood.

When I played in the All-Star Game, everything began to intensify. First, there were two All-Star Games that top recruits could select. So, naturally, I chose the Cali-Florida game because I assumed I would go to USC. But now, my motivation was different; to prove USC wrong for rejecting me.

As I prepared to travel to the game, two planes left the area, the Central Florida plane and the South Florida plane. The coaches were from nearby, so we rode together. Who would believe I just so happened to get the seat next to the Linebackers Coach for our team? What are the chances? I sat beside him, eager to make a good impression before the big game. He had other thoughts in mind.

For the entire flight, he could not stop telling me how eager he was to coach Bruce Mompremier. That was the name that kept coming out of his mouth. Not Brandon Siler. Bruce Mompremier. For five hours, that's all I heard: "He has such a great work ethic." "His instincts are impeccable." "He's gonna make a great college linebacker." To add insult to injury, the coach didn't even get my name right. He repeatedly called me "Silas." Ironically, he could say "Mompremier" but not "Siler." At the beginning of the flight, I was stewing, by the time we got off the plane, I was boiling.

With Bruce starting ahead of me, I was miserable. I kept correcting the coach when he called me "Silas"; he would defiantly yell, "I'll call you whatever I want to, son!" The ambition began to rise in me. I paused after one drill and told the coach, "By the end of this week, you're gonna know my name...." I would outperform Bruce in drills and on the field, but the coach would only praise him. I was frustrated.

After a couple of days, I was discouraged. I called my mom every day and would tell her, "Hey, I'm just going to go to one of those other All-Star games. I'm sick of this." She would reply, "Son, you're not gonna like what people do to you in life, but you must stick it out." The rejection was like a war on my already unstable mind.

On game day, I let all that aggression out on the field. While I wasn't starting at Linebacker, I was on the Special Teams unit. The second my cleats hit the football field, I was screaming, "Kick the damn ball off! I'm bout to kill whoever touches it!" While I was supposed to be on the sideline for a T.V. reset, I was on the field screaming at whoever would listen. The Cali Team was staring at me as I yelled at them. "Get back out here so I can hit somebody!" Everyone thought I was crazy.

The second the returner touched the ball; I slammed him down just like I said I would. After a few plays, they threw the ball, and I caught an interception in the flats. I was 30 yards away from scoring, but I wanted them to feel me instead. I ran diagonally across the field and ran at the quarterback in a rage to run him over. When I got to my feet, I realized I had just blown my chance to score a touchdown in the All-Star game. Later in the game, I was covering a kick, and an opposing player pushed me in the back on the opponent's sideline. I quickly jumped to my feet, trying to fight the other team, telling them, "I'm gonna make y'all pay for that." On the next drive, I had another interception that I ran back for a touchdown.

The second I stepped in the end zone, I kept running back to their sideline and spiked the ball in the middle of their team, screaming, "I told y'all I would make you pay. I TOLD Y'ALL!"

I ran back to my sideline, and right before I got there, I saw that Linebacker Coach. He was pointing in the air as if to signal me to give him a chest bump. Right before I went to jump, I stopped on a dime. "Hey! What's my name!?" He said, "Siler! Siler!" I said, "I told you you're gonna know my name!" Despite my antics, my play on the field was undeniable. I won MVP of that game and celebrated with my team.

The day I returned home, my first call was from Coach Lane Kiffin. I cussed him out and hung up on him. I was officially opening my recruitment back up again.

I've grown quite a bit since my teenage years, but those recruiting days taught me what the wrong fuel could do to a leader. My fuel during that time was anger, driven by my confusion about all the trauma I faced and my strange relationship with God. Sidenote, I didn't know what I believed. My mom was a Christian; my stepdad was an on-again/off-again Five Percenter, and I believed in reincarnation. I was a ball of confusion. More on that later.

This lack of grounding led me to root my decisions in vengeance and the need to prove others wrong, rather than to see my vision become a reality. Don't get me wrong; I was still successful. I was the best at what I did for a reason. But being the best isn't always healthy.

I learned early on that you can accomplish so much, even with bad intentions. Still, the improper motive will eventually destroy the soul of its host. I have met many leaders who wanted to accomplish something great. But, their motivation was driven by bitterness or vengeance. They are externally successful, with all the accomplishments that anyone would like, but internally they are traumatized. The fuel of hatred was slowly poisoning them.

I was growing, learning, succeeding, and winning, but my misguided motives began to poison my soul. As soon as I stepped foot on the campus at the University of Florida, I knew something was off.

Unfortunately, I wasn't prepared for what I would discover while I was there. I had spent all these years trying to escape, but I couldn't escape myself.

CHAPTER SIX

LEADING FROM THE MIDDLE

Synopsis: All leaders are not at the front when they start leading. Most of them are not even at the front when they begin leading. Brandon encountered this in his first year at the University of Florida. He shares how his life changed and how he learned to lead in spaces where he was not yet #1.

There is no place in college football quite like the University of Florida in the Southeastern Conference. I know what you're thinking, "Of course, YOU would say that." I challenge anyone to prove me wrong. With 90,000 fans in a tightly constructed stadium' on top of the Florida heat, we call this place "The Swamp" for a reason. Few colleges or NFL environments can match the ambiance. I dreamt of playing football in a place like that, but Florida caught me off guard. One thing I knew for sure was that my mom loved Coach Ron Zook. Coach Zook was a hard-nosed, defensive-minded coach who was far different from the flash and dash of Coach Steve Spurrier, his legendary predecessor.

Coach Zook quickly impressed my mom. College coaches only get one official visit to a recruit's residence. They understand that visits must pay dividends. Sure, Coach Zook was a skilled recruiter, but he seemed like he genuinely cared. His presence disarmed my momma's skepticism and made her trust his leadership. I'll never forget them laughing and joking like best friends. After she met Coach Zook, my recruitment was still open, but it was already closed in her mind. Another SEC head coach visited, and my mom refused to go out of her bedroom to see him. She kept saying she was "tired," which meant, "Boy, you're going to Florida with Coach Zook."

Ultimately, it was my choice. It didn't hurt that, around that time, my baby sister Jada was born. I saw her as a precious gem I could love and protect as a big brother. She would need positive influences that weren't in Pine Hills, so I decided to stay as close to her as possible. I still felt responsible for loving my family and bringing them with me on this journey toward my ultimate vision.

When I stepped onto the University of Florida campus, I was ready to face the world's challenges with the same passion I used to tackle running backs and quarterbacks. I entered that first year feeling highly confident in myself. How hard could this be? After all, this was my vision, and I had every resource necessary to make it a reality.

Unfortunately, I quickly realized that this would be more challenging than I expected. I ran into a series of brick walls.

Part of my vision for myself was contingent on leaving college, with my degree, in just three years. I knew that if I wanted to take care of my family and get them out of that harsh environment, I needed to get to the next stage of my vision immediately. I remember hearing Coach Zook say, "If you bring me a few more recruits like you, we'll win a national championship in your 3rd year here." I was determined not to become stuck in this city, no matter what it took. With that in mind, I instructed my academic counselor to build my schedule around the idea that I would graduate from Florida in three years. I decided to get my degree quickly and make my way to the NFL Draft, poised to be the next great linebacker in the league. Imagine a freshman athlete asking for more classes when he hits campus. Imagine the passion for 18 hours a day, having multiple two-a-day practices and a budding social life. I shake my head thinking about how idealistic I was to race toward completing my vision. Then, just as my confidence rose, I hit "the walls."

My first wall was cultural. I was entirely unprepared for the campus atmosphere. Strip away all my athletic abilities and physical stature, and I was just a kid from the projects trying to make something of my life. As compelling as my narrative was, it was just one of the thousands of stories in Gainesville and a hundred on the football team. Culturally, not everyone on the football team saw a championship as essential to their stories. In addition, I was used to being on teams with an established sense of camaraderie and brotherhood. This family feeling was completely absent when I arrived at Florida. Slowly, I began to drift, dreaming of being back home.

One of the former players on the team, Tony George, saw that I was a "fish out of water" and decided to help. Thank God for him. He understood where I came from and decided to connect me with some people who had a similar background and life experience. He introduced me to a local guy named Torie, and I truly felt at home with him, his friends, and his family. We would cook crabs and play cards and dominoes. It was a slice of Pine Hills in Gainesville, but feeling "like a fish out of water" wasn't the only brick wall I encountered.

The football reality hit me like a mac truck as well. I was expecting to join the team as an all-world linebacker. I had all the bravado and swagger of a young all-star recruit, but when I arrived, I faced another rude awakening. At that time, Channing Crowder was the starting "Mike Linebacker" or Middle Linebacker in the defensive scheme. Crowder was the starter, and the coaches put Javier Estopinan in front of me on the depth chart. Shocked, I found myself third in the pecking order and out of a regular rotation on the field.

Was this déjà vu? I was further back in the depth chart than I ever expected. Like the Cali-Florida game, I was angry, but more sad than upset this time. I called my mom all the time to complain about my plight. "They don't believe in me. They got these guys ahead of me. I just need an opportunity. I'm done!" As she did in high school, my mom encouraged me with advice and love. She would not let me quit. She challenged me to continue and fight, regardless of what people did and how I felt. I started working harder, remembering my vision as a kid, and refused to take "no" for an answer. Eventually, I was able to beat out Javier on the depth chart. The coaches could see my work ethic and my heart.

Like the Cali-Florida game, I played on special teams, giving my all on every kickoff and blowing up returners with lightning speed. While working my tail off in practice, Channing Crowder sang my praises. At the time, he was an All-SEC linebacker poised to be a high NFL draft pick, so his word carried weight in the locker room. Behind closed doors, he told the defensive coaches I deserved to play next to him in the defensive scheme. He was convinced I was better than the man next to him. Channing was looking out for me, and I was in awe of his confidence. Unfortunately, the story has a plot twist. Instead of replacing the other linebacker, I ended up replacing him. Right before the game against one of our arch-rivals, The Georgia Bulldogs, Channing got hurt. He was due to be out for a few games, which sent our fanbase into a tailspin. Channing was a veteran on our team, this was a big blow to our confidence. The fans, and even some of the players, wondered if we would have the ability to stabilize the defense with such a significant loss.

While others panicked, I knew that this was my opportunity. I had quietly observed that something needed to change in our defensive leadership. I saw what needed to happen earlier in the season against Mississippi State. The running back for State, Jerious Norwood, ran our defense ragged, racking up almost 200 yards in a significant, season-defining loss. I was still learning, but I knew we were a far better team than they were, but we couldn't pull out the victory. You know something has gone wrong whenever you give up that many rushing yards. Looking at the box score, I saw that Channing had 22 tackles in that game, breaking a school record. To many, that was a heroic achievement, but from the sideline, my ears perked up as I watched him pad his stats. I was one of the only guys on the field who could recognize what was happening.

While he played the hero on the field, Channing let the Mississippi State backs run through his opening in the scheme and then rushed back into view to make the tackle. He was letting them chew up yards on our team so that he could look good. Those nine or ten yard bursts overrode anything he did with the record-breaking tackles.

To make matters worse, he embarrassed the defensive line after the game. He stood up and yelled that he was "the only one tackling" on the field. Something caught my eye as I watched him berate our teammates. As a budding leader, I watched how the players reacted. Players like Jarvis Moss and Ray McDonald shrank to an almost childlike form. They were down on themselves. It's funny to think about this now, because some of these players would eventually become legends in Gator lore. It's hard to imagine anything moving these vigorous young men. Still, at that moment, they were rendered weak by embarrassing criticism.

In my own community growing up, I watched what other people did wrong and tried to create a reality that helped me do the opposite of everything I saw. Every vision requires a counter-idea, a way of seeing the counterproductive practices of others and doing the exact opposite. At the time, there was little I could do to change the reality of what I saw. Our defense needed leaders. Our team required leaders. I was crazy enough to believe that I, a freshman, could be one of them.

The second that Channing was injured, my chance to reform the defense came swiftly. I'll never forget that first time I ran into the huddle and stared across at the defense. I took a deep breath and looked them in the eyes. "Listen, y'all are ten times better than these fools across the ball. I don't care if you're supposed to go an A-Gap or a B-Gap. Slip into a D-Gap or a C-Gap. I don't care!" I said, almost breathing fire. "You beat their ass because you're better than them. And if you happen to be in the wrong gap, guess what? I'm five yards behind you, and I'll make it right. READY, BREAK?" I clapped and walked away from the huddle. Before I turned my back, I could see their collective shock. They looked at me as if they had seen a ghost.

The defensive line got down in their stances, looked over their shoulder, and laughed with a "Who is this kid?" tone. Then, when the ball was snapped, I did exactly what I told them I would do. I let them do some things they weren't allowed to do, and when it came time to accept the blame, I took it all.

Motivated by memories of my childhood dreams, I dedicated myself to working harder and refused to accept "no" as an answer.

We immediately improved on defense. The front seven started to gel and play as a unit. To my surprise, I began to receive conference attention and national acclaim. Everything was coming together, and then Channing came back into the lineup. At this point, they were sour about him coming back. They preferred my style and were reaping the benefits with better play from our defense. I believed in them and allowed them to do certain things that I knew they could do. I never talked down to them, but only spoke well of them and lifted their spirits.

The moment Crowder returned, the coaches knew they had to adjust. I stayed at Mike Linebacker, and he moved to the Sam Linebacker position. The defense was happy, but obviously, Channing was not, and this decision quickly ruined our relationship. He was the guy who took me on my recruiting visit, the one who showed me the ins and outs of campus and guided me through the process. When it came to losing his spot, Channing was no longer a fan. Whatever friendship we had quickly disintegrated.

When the media would ask me about the shift, I played the long game, understanding the gravity of the situation. "Channing Crowder is one of the greatest linebackers in the history of this school." I would give him credit when they asked why I took his spot. "Channing taught me so much; I'm trying to live up to that example and do what I can." Unfortunately, while I saw the big picture, Coach Zook did not have the same tact that I did with the media. Instead of acknowledging Channing, he generously praised me. "Well, I believe Brandon Siler is one of the greatest linebackers this campus has ever seen. He's going to be even better than Channing is." The Gators fan base was elated because they could see the hope of a future juggernaut on the defense, but Coach Zook had severed our friendship. One day, I walked into our defensive coordinator's office and saw a quote on the whiteboard. Someone had taken a sharpie and written, "We don't need Channing. We've got Siler." I looked at Coach Strong, "Who wrote this?" He shook his head and stared at me, "Who do you think? Channing."

The statement is true, "Long live our idols. May they never be our rivals."

I started half the season as a freshman. Then, I was the SEC Freshman Player of the Year, a massive accomplishment I had difficulty believing. I was the best freshman, in the best conference, in college football. Out of every recruit, I was able to make an immediate impact.

Shortly after that, Channing went to the league, and the Gators fired Coach Zook in the middle of the season. I was enraged by that decision and even told others I was displeased. To be fired in the middle of the season felt excessive and ridiculous. I never felt like they gave him a genuine chance. "If you get me a couple of other recruits, we'll win a championship in your 3rd year." Eventually, this turned out to be true.

The university hired up-and-coming head coach, Urban Meyer, from the University of Utah. At the time, I was a diehard Zook fan. After all, he was like family to my family. I was skeptical of what Coach Meyer could do in the SEC. However, I sensed that Coach Meyer knew what he needed to do to stabilize what could be a volatile situation. His leadership style is unconventional and rooted in the idea of building a family among the team. He could see that I was one of his top athletes. Plus, I was a 4.0 student and won SEC Freshman Player of the Year. I was the poster child.

In the first meeting he had as a coach, he did something strategic. The team was largely closed off to his approach and wasn't trying to hear what he had to say. At the beginning of the meeting, he said, "Look, I am not like the coaches you've had in the past. I won't lie to you. I won't treat everyone the same. I'll treat my superstars like superstars and my shit like shit. If you don't like that, then find a way to make yourself a superstar so I can change how I treat you." I could respect that because I knew every player wouldn't be treated equally. Everyone knows that you don't treat all the players the same.

He also repeatedly said, "We need a team full of Brandon Silers." I couldn't believe what I heard. I sat in my seat, confused. I didn't know this man from anywhere, and I was a far bigger fan of Coach Zook. "We need a team full of Brandon Silers." Three times in the meeting, he said that. My teammates looked at me like I was crazy. They were convinced that I was an enemy of Coach Meyer and couldn't understand why I was being praised like this. Was I lying to them or tricking them into believing something while playing both sides? I had never spoke to Coach Meyer before he said that, but he used this as an opportunity to display his leadership genius. I began to feel the weight of separation.

Channing and some other former players would return to campus to host parties. They would invite the entire team except me. They would talk with each of my teammates, but not me. I would walk into a crowd of teammates at a function, and they would disperse because of me.

It made me feel like an outcast. He separated me from the other guys so that I would be one of his guys. During the entire second year, I dealt with the former players coming back and telling my teammates everything they thought about me. "This dude is snitching on everyone to the coach." It didn't make sense. I would throw parties and drink with the best of them, but some teammates actually believed it. Whenever I got into that situation, I was forced into fight or flight mode. That entire year, I knew I had to fight. I fought for my place to belong. I fought physically too. I struggled with my identity, just as Meyer struggled to establish his identity with the team.

I was struggling to find myself, and my struggle was about to worsen. I didn't know much about mental health at this point, but I look back now and realize that mine was rapidly deteriorating. Then, "it" happened. I tried to take my own life.

CHAPTER SEVEN

LEADING WHILE BROKEN

Synopsis: In this chapter, Brandon bares his soul about leading from a broken place of mental health during his college success. What do you do when you are broken mentally but still have to appear strong?

People always used to tell me that I looked like my dad. I know that's a cliché for some, but in my case, it's true. I am the spitting image of my father. Our voice, walk, build, and smile are all identical. I used to resent that to the core. After all, we lived in the same city when I was a kid, and he refused to acknowledge me. He would never come to my games or take me anywhere. The disappointment and anger from his rejection had driven me to that point. Imagine my surprise when he walked onto the University of Florida practice field.

I heard his voice first. We were in the middle of our drills, and I picked up a familiar sound echoing out in the air. "Wait, that sounds like my voice." I spun around and saw him walking on the field with arms outstretched. What?? My shock quickly turned to confusion. This was a closed practice. How did he get here? How did he get through the fence? Who let him in? What is he doing here?

An avalanche of anger followed the flood of questions as I realized what he was trying to do. He saw my moments of success the year before, winning SEC Freshman Player of the Year and leading a defense as a freshman. He showed up right at the height of my public attention to get a piece of the credit for all I had accomplished. I was there without him, and he wanted to join in after the fact. I wasn't having that!

After the incident, everyone could see how much it affected me. To say I was enraged would be putting it mildly. I found the security team and angrily interrogated them. When I returned to my senses, I understood how easy it would be to let my "twin" onto the field. No one understood how much I yearned for my father to be present in my life. I was empty and needed the affirmation that only my dad could give. Yet, despite my deepest longing, he never spoke to me or invested in a son he could be proud of. And now he was in my face, close to me, after all these years. How selfish can a man be?

He had done this emergence out of nowhere before. He tried to come around when I was a high school football player. He showed up at one football game and stood near the end zone, making himself seen and known that I was his son. I spotted him from afar and lost it. I took an interception back for a touchdown and spiked the ball as hard as possible while I stared him down. This moment felt like Déjà vu with anger, sadness, and depression.

At this point, I did not know anything about mental health and the effects that extreme depression can have on your mind and body. After the incident with my father, I spiraled. No one knew, but I decided that none of this was worth living for anymore.

So, I grabbed a bottle of pills and swallowed them all.

When I regained consciousness, I looked up at Pam and Coach Meyer. They had been looking for me, and the only reason I'm here today is that they found me and rushed me to the hospital. The two loudest voices in my life at the time had saved my life. Finally, Coach Meyer and Pam experienced their realization. It looked like I had everything together, but I was broken. Just because I had all the answers, didn't mean I wasn't facing things that were greater than me. They saw me at my lowest point and still believed in me long after returning to reality.

I learned that belief is not just a quality leaders must display to those around them. It is also something that every leader needs to function at their best. The ultimate leader can develop others in a way that connects them to their vulnerability. The ultimate leader is also able to connect the people that are around him to their ultimate motivation. Everyone needs to understand what makes you "go." Why are you working so hard? What makes you want to achieve? What hurts you? What drives you? Pam and Coach Meyer understood more about me, at that moment, than they ever had before, helping me shape my future. There's an art to following and leading followers into being the best followers.

Reaching this point was my first wake-up call to take mental health seriously. It was an alarm I would ignore until God forced me to deal with it. At this moment, I confronted the reality that no matter how much I wanted to ignore it, my dad is my dad. It would be easy to bury his influence in my life and minimize its effects on my psyche. There was no way around it. For better or for worse, that's my father.

I took some consolation in the fact that even though we look alike, act alike, move alike, and talk alike, our core values could not be more different. Core values are the fundamental elements of what is deep inside yourself. It's what makes you move and helps you decide to live a certain way. Unfortunately, his core values caused him to prioritize his rap career over his children. He ignored me in plain sight and showed up almost two decades too late. I resolved that my core values must be different. My core values are the things that make me show up for my kids and sacrifice doing what I want to do for the things that will benefit my future.

A leader cannot effectively lead without understanding the individuals they are responsible for guiding.

I led my family and this team from a better place than I had experienced. During my sophomore year, we were struggling on and off the field. Our team lost all our games under 2:15 in the 4th quarter. We had talent and experience, but the difference between good and great is in the fine details. The little things you don't expect can create wins, losses, and even championships. That little seal block, those moments where you run the scheme to perfection, the chances you take advantage of when the other team makes a mistake, make great teams great. My second year was all about the team learning what greatness required.

As I transitioned to my Junior Year, the mood around the campus began to change quickly. The arrival of a 6'3" freshman quarterback captivated the fan base in ways we'd never seen. Alumni welcomed him with open arms. Friends and family would incessantly ask about him. They wanted to know if this kid could make it. I had my doubts. A homeschooled, proper Christian quarterback? In this locker room? There was no way that he would lead this team. As soon as he stepped on campus, I sized him up.

Coach Meyer knew that I was the partier and party organizer. I had strict instructions from him while he was visiting UF: "Don't go near Tim Tebow." Urban said. Yet, I decided to test that rule out. The morning after a legendary party, on a recruiting weekend, we were having breakfast with the entire team, the recruits, and their parents. I made a beeline toward him in front of the whole team. I could feel Meyer staring at me while I approached him and said, "So, you the motherfucker they call Tim Tebow, huh?" To my surprise, his entire family burst out in laughter. These were real people, just like the rest of us, and I continued introducing myself to his entire family. Subsequently, Urban told me all the wrong times for the rest of the events during his visit, and that was my last encounter until he arrived on campus.

On the recruit's first day on campus, I received a phone call, "Can I speak to B-Si?" "Yeah, who's this?" "Tim Tebow" "Hey, what's up, Tim?" "I was just calling to see if I can hang with you?" In my mind, I felt like Tim had heard that I was a partier and was ready to spring into the wild, crazy life of a college student. Between the time I introduced myself and now, I had learned about his family's immense devotion to God. Why would he call me to hang out unless he wanted to experience something different? I was a bit confused, but I reluctantly drove to the dorm room, picked him up on my scooter, and took him over to my place.

That night, we played video games, and no matter how he tried, he couldn't beat me. In his book, he said he was beating me that night, but I don't remember it that way. I had a party scheduled right after hanging with him. When he found out the party was happening, Tim spoke up. "Well, I'll hang with you if you don't mind." "Of course, I thought, this sheltered homeschool kid was ready to get after it. He's finally free." He rolled with me. I'm getting everybody into the party, and everybody's with me. As soon as we got to the party, I realized that this was not the typical party kid. Tim came to watch me and connect with the team, but he didn't do anything that we did. He never drank, smoked, or messed around with girls. He just wanted to learn how to lead.

When we entered the club, everyone inside was going crazy over Tim being there. It was as if Justin Bieber had just walked into the club, and Tim hadn't even played one down. It was one of the most insane reactions to someone I had experienced at this point, and after about 30 minutes, I was over it. I took Tim behind the bar, and went to the dance floor. A young lady approached me, leaned in, and said, "Hey, are you that guy?" I smiled. "Of course, I am!" To my surprise, she said, "You're the guy who came with Tim Tebow, right?" What?? Here I am, the star middle linebacker and poster child for Florida football, and now, I was the guy who came with Tim Tebow. That was the first and last time I let him accompany me to a party.

I realized that Tim was an incredible leader in the making. He had determination, a work ethic, intuitive skills, and even a mean streak. But there was something different about him. He believed in God. Until now, I had only seen Pam consistently living out her faith in front of others. Tim was just as consistent. He was the one who disproved my pushup theory. Remember when I used to think that if I did the same pushups as someone else, I would beat them because I had more inside of me? Not with Tim. He could do the work, and then he still had something extra. His God factor fueled him. And he was watching me, which was a small picture of why I was the team leader. I ultimately became the leader of the football team because I could relate to every person who was there. When Coach Meyer arrived, he quickly realized that the group had different fractions. Different subgroups had their own distinct identities. Yet, somehow, I related to all of them. I could relate to the geeks, thugs, and country boys. I could also relate to the partiers and drinkers.

Wherever I was, Tebow was close behind me. We would play video games together, eat together, and lift together. Whatever I lifted, he lifted the same. He would always slide into the cold tub right next to me, he was determined to do whatever it took to be a leader worth following on this team. And to my surprise, he was the real deal.

I quickly realized that there was only one way to eliminate the subgroups: Be able to relate to them all. My typical after-practice activities meant I was in study hall until 8:30 to connect with the nerds. After spending substantial time with them, I hung out with the smokers and drinkers until 10:30, and then I went to the best parties to connect with them. After the night, I would wake up at dawn to go fishing with the country boys. I was everywhere, and I knew I had to be. If we were to have any success, I knew it rested on my shoulders.

Tebow gravitated to me because he knew he couldn't relate to everyone, but he was trying to figure out how I did it. It was natural to me because I recognized that's what a leader does.

A leader can only lead if he understands the people he's teaching. So, I knew there were times for the gentle approach and tough love. There were even times when we needed to fight it out.

That year a pair of younger players were firmly entrenched in a beef. One was a running back, and the other was a wide receiver. Their veiled threats and hatred were boiling, especially when the wide receiver's family came to town. He had been telling them what the running back was doing, and they decided they would handle it as a unit. They were all riding in the car and saw the running back walking through the campus. He, his cousin, and his sister jumped out of the car and started chasing him on campus. Eventually, he got away, but that was the same night I called a mandatory party for the team.

After every team member was there except for the two of them, I called them individually. Neither one of them wanted to show up. "Listen, if y'all don't come to this party, Imma beat yo ass. I don't care what the problem is. You've got 30 minutes to join your team, or I'm coming to find you."

Tebow and I played video games with all the other players in the house. Of course, I was winning, and I lost track of time. Eventually, I realized the place was empty except for the two of us. I walk outside, and these two guys pulled up, arguing and going back and forth. I go downstairs and say, "Look, first of all, we need to understand that it's a brotherhood on this campus. No one's family can arrive on this campus and jump out on one of our teammates. If that happens again, I'll beat the shit out of anyone who does it."

I continued looking at the two players at the center of the conflict, "You've got a problem with him. And you've got a problem with him. Yea? Okay, cool, so here's what we're going to do. Nobody else jumps into this, or I'm jumping in on the other side. Y'all two fight it out right now." A hush came over the team. The two players looked at each other and then at me. "Y'all heard what I said! Fight it out, or I'll fight you both!"

I'm unsure who threw the first punch, but they started swinging at each other. The months of animosity were being worked out in real-time with the entire team here to see it. At one point, the wide receiver's sister tried to jump in, and we had to throw her out of the circle.

"Nope, no one is allowed to jump in.", I said. After they were too tired to swing anymore, I stepped in and pulled them apart. "Y'all good, right?? All right, now y'all go'on, and hug this shit out. And we don't speak about this anymore from this day forward, okay?" After the incident, I sent everyone back into the house, and we partied like it never happened. The next day, the running back and wide receiver were spotting each other in the gym, and their conflict was never spoken of again.

That was one of the striking moments when I knew this team was exceptional. I knew something about them could achieve greatness if they were willing to buy in, love one another, become a family, and do the little things well. As a leader, you often see what others can do before they can see it themselves. You know what they can do and who they can be before they have that understanding and belief.

I saw it in the 2006 Florida Gators team. I just had to continue believing for them to catch up. I had a feeling that if they caught up in time, we might be able to win big. My vision might ultimately come true.

CHAPTER EIGHT

"DON'T TALK ABOUT IT. BE ABOUT IT"

Synopsis: What happens when you demand greatness from others and refuse to take "no" for an answer? In his national championship season, Brandon experiences the peak of being a successful leader.

"Y'all are full of shit!"

On October 14, 2006, I exploded on my team. From the first day I closed my eyes and saw the vision of my life, I had a plan. During my high school years, I aimed to get recruited to a Division 1 school, lead that team, and win the national championship in my third year. This vision never wavered. My sophomore year was filled with a few close losses and a shift to the new coaching culture under Urban Meyer. We demanded more than a 9-3 record because we had a vision for greater success.

On this day, I was fed up. We had incredible talent, strong coaching, and outstanding leadership, yet we lost a game we never should have. Auburn beat us 27-17, and I felt the vision slipping slightly from my grasp. I refused to let that happen.

Sometimes, a leader needs to gently and calmly guide a team to perform their best, and there are other times when shocking their system is necessary. And on this day, it was all about shock. To begin with, I was shocked that we even lost to this team. Why were we losing to Auburn? We were far superior to them. Why did we continue to make the same mistakes as last year? What was wrong with our offense? As I rocked back and forth for 10 minutes, my frustration slowly boiled over.

"Offense! Y'all lost this game for us!" I started pointing out specific players in the locker room who weren't fulfilling their positions, and I dared them to tell me otherwise. We all knew the truth. Some of the coaches felt the tension rising and said, "We need to stop this." Coach Meyer stepped in and said, "Let this shit happen! Give it to 'em, Siler! Tell them why we lost!" Hearing Coach Meyer endorse my outburst fueled my rage. I screamed, swung my helmet, and got in their faces. If anyone had anything to say that day, I was ready to address it immediately.

The faces of my teammates and coaches displayed a mixture of shock, confusion, and determination. I vividly remember each face, including those of my successor Brandon Spikes and the future leader Tim Tebow. That day, something shifted for our team. We finally embraced the passion required to achieve greatness. From that moment on, everyone understood that they needed to be fully committed.

I knew we had the potential for greatness before that moment, but I had questions. In my sophomore year, the team was good until we were required to do the little things: the blocks, the seals, and the attention to detail. Those little things were missing.

Ultimately, I was mostly concerned about our effort. As a leader, talent matters, but effort always matters more than raw ability. We had talent but needed more effort to be great. We needed to come together and have consistent leadership.

Coach Meyer formed the leadership group, consisting of people who were not necessarily the best players, but had influence over different cliques on the team. We had a mixture of diverse cultures and people groups, which Urban realized was entirely different from his experience at Utah. We needed to unite, but sometimes we were not on the same page. Initially, few people spoke during the sub-group meetings.

Coach Meyer was an old-school coach, meaning his methods were direct, and his workouts were brutal. Before that season started, the coaches put us through workouts designed to improve us and see who would quit. We were ordered to touch every stadium step, followed by core training with legs in the air. If even one person dropped their legs, the coach would blow the whistle, and we had to start over.

One of my teammates didn't get the memo. He kept slacking off and putting his feet down, thinking no one could see him. He wasn't hurting; he was being lazy. I was tired of repeating the drill over and over again. After telling him twice to tighten up, I took it a step further. I stood up, slapped him in the face, and screamed at him to tighten up. The team fell silent, waiting to see how the coaches would respond. They just blew the whistle and instructed us to start over. This time, we performed the drill perfectly.

After this workout, we had a contentious leadership meeting. Some of the other team leaders indirectly expressed their feelings and complaints. Our coach asked us, "What are some things you're struggling with or don't like?" One of my teammates said, "Well...I don't like when guys show off in front of coaches." We all agreed. Of course, we were bothered by that too. Another teammate chimed in, saying, "Yeah, like you don't have to be putting your hands all over people just to act tough." At that point, I realized they were talking about me.

"Hold on now...Listen, where I come from, when you take your hand and put it on another human being, that's when you're ready to do what it takes." I continued speaking but stood up so that they would feel my presence. "You guys want to act like you're from the hood by sagging your pants, wearing your hair nappy, and smoking weed. That's fake! I know where I'm from, and I'm secure in that. And if anyone thinks that's fake, they can meet me outside. We'll resolve that now. Bet you won't think that's fake anymore." The coach tried to stop me from walking out, but I insisted.

"No, I'll be outside. And if any of you think I'm fake, I'll be waiting for you." I stood outside, waiting for company, but no one came. As they left the building, I said, "I guess no one thinks I'm fake, huh?" and walked away. At that moment, I had to show them that toughness cannot be fabricated. I was real and always prepared because I was secure in myself.

No matter how much talent we knew we had, I had doubts about the offense that Coach Meyer was running. As a leader, doubt is inevitable, but you have to find ways to motivate and inspire even those you doubt.

I was always aware of my responsibility. I wasn't the leader in my first year of college, but after that, I understood my role as the person who set the tone. Leading a talented group of people to greatness can be intimidating if you're not prepared to sacrifice. I was willing to endure discomfort to achieve greatness. I was ready to be singled out, ostracized, and treated differently. I didn't need everyone to like me; I needed respect.

Recently, someone asked me, "What has changed about college football today compared to when you played?" The question made me pause. I never want to undermine the act of getting out there on the football field and putting your entire body on the line. Today's college football athletes are gifted and prepare themselves from a young age. However, during our time, we trained to be warriors. We trained to be different and ready for battle. Many outstanding college football athletes of our time, and even of all time, struggled to succeed in the NFL. The hunger required to survive, sets us apart from professional athletes. Making a college football roster and earning a Division 1 scholarship is a miraculous achievement according to the percentages. It demands fierce determination and desire. Today, the atmosphere of the game is different, and entitlement is more prevalent in sports.

After Coach Meyer arrived in Florida, we established traditions of midnight lifts, infamous brutal drills, and a mindset of "kill or be killed" on the field. We used to run drills where the only rule was to get the ball; other than that, there were no rules. I used to choke people until they slept. I loved it. The Gator greats loved those moments. I cherished the midnight practices and the chance to challenge one another physically. Tim Tebow loved every second of it too. However, those days are gone, and coaches would be fired for some of the drills we used to run every week.

Because the game has a different ethos, leadership has changed too. As a leader, you built ultimate warriors who would do anything for you, no matter the cost. They would do it simply because they believe. This was our strategy, and that's why we were such a successful team.

Can you motivate someone to run through a wall without knowing what's on the other side? Can you inspire people to put their livelihood and reputation on the line for something greater than themselves? This is the test of leadership. I was ruthlessly committed to it.

I learned that to lead, I would need to train as if going to war. I'll never forget when one of the younger linebackers said, "Why are y'all training so hard? We're just tackling someone. It's not that serious." He didn't see what I saw. I knew it was serious if we were going to reach our potential. I knew we needed to be inspired during moments of doubt and uncertainty, knowing our leaders had adequately prepared themselves to face anything. No, we were not literally going into battle, but if we prepared as if we were, nothing could hold us down. Leadership is more than just doing your job well; it's about setting the tone.

I didn't complain about the dangerous heat and bright sun during our early morning workouts. I changed the atmosphere for our team. Instead of saying, "Damn, it's hot out here!" I said, "It's a great day in Florida, baby. That's why only Florida boys can play here!" Of course, it was scorching hot, and I wanted to leave just like everyone else, but I never wanted to show any signs of weakness in front of the guys I was leading on the field. People were always watching me.

... Achieving such a desired goal also sparked a desire for more...

At a certain point, the players on our team didn't even feel comfortable complaining in front of me. I loved that. The fact that they couldn't come around and have the same conversations when I was present meant, they understood the standard that came with having my attention. If people feel comfortable complaining around you, then you are too familiar with them. I refused to participate in that. I spoke the truth and called us to higher standards every time. That's the expectation that comes with having my attention.

One of the adjustments I made during the season was using motivational tactics. I decided to motivate the team during the season through a special chain. I wore this chain around campus, and Coach Meyer couldn't stand it. My conviction was simple: to win, we needed every person to be a vital link in the chain. We were only as strong as our weakest link. I wore a massive chain around campus and added players' names to it only if I felt they were strong enough to be our weakest link. It openly communicated with those who needed to step up their game. Urban knew that psychologically, we should try to get everyone onto the chain as soon as possible, but I disagreed. The battle of who belonged on the chain was a frequent point of contention between Urban and me.

I wasn't unfair to the idea. They could make their way onto the chain whenever someone earned their place. Ultimately, everyone bought into the vision. Urban knew how stubborn I was when I strongly believed in something. He knew he wouldn't be able to talk me out of it. Nobody was going to stop me, and everyone understood that. Ultimately, even Urban bought into the chain. And we began to see results.

Two weeks after the loss to Auburn, our season started falling into place. Despite the diverse cultures and internal challenges, the team rallied together. We began to find our resilience. It was as though our leadership finally resonated with them. Though we had some close calls, such as a narrow victory against our archrival Georgia and a challenging game against Vanderbilt, we qualified for the SEC Championship game. We were cautiously optimistic about what was possible.

Against Arkansas, we knew they had a potent rushing attack with Darren McFadden and Felix Jones. Commentators seemed convinced we would be dominated on the ground, but we knew better. I was ready to prove just how formidable our defense could be. We held their rushing attack to 130 yards, and I had 12 total tackles to lead us to victory. Our offense finally clicked, scoring 38 points with dynamic running and big passing plays. With this win, we qualified for the National Championship game.

As we prepared for the National Championship game, we started hearing talk about our upcoming opponent, Ohio State. Commentators loved the classic North-South matchup, and this one was highly anticipated by all college football fans. The Buckeyes were led by Heisman Trophy-winning quarterback, Troy Smith, who was elusive, athletic, and an unflappable leader. With Ted Ginn Jr., as their wide receiver, and a tough defense, we knew they were a real opponent. However, something was different about our team.

In the weeks leading up to the game, we were all business. Everyone's dream we had all worked towards for the past two years was within our grasp. We had transformed into a different team compared to the Auburn game, and it was time to show the world what we could accomplish. I heard all the chatter, but the reporters were exaggerating.

"What are you going to do about Troy Smith?"
"Does their speed concern you?"
"What will your defense do to contain their offense?"

These were the questions and comments I heard repeatedly. Urban had a strict rule that we couldn't provide any "bulletin board material" for that game. At one point, I found myself alone in front of 50 TV cameras. The very first question they asked me was, "Hey Brandon, are you more afraid of Troy Smith's arms or his legs?"

I nearly lost my mind. Taking a deep breath, I smiled and replied, "We're not afraid of Troy Smith at all. Yes, he's a good player, and y'all can say whatever you want, but don't get it twisted. We ain't scared at all!" It was time to make a statement.

When game day arrived, I felt more hyped than ever before. We were ready for whatever they threw at us. Our coaches had devised the game plan, and each player believed in themselves to the maximum extent.

The crowd was electric as we kicked the ball off to Ohio State. The defense was jumping on the sidelines, eager to step onto the field. Then it happened. Tedd Ginn returned the opening kickoff 100 yards for a touchdown. It happened so quickly, yet time seemed to slow down. The Buckeyes held Reggie Nelson, creating a huge lane, but the refs missed it. Once Ginn gained a step, it was over.

I was standing next to Coach Meyer, who was irate. He screamed, cursed, and threw his headset down. Before the game, I had told him that we would easily win as long as our offense could score because their team wouldn't score on us. In that moment of confusion, he panicked. I knew I needed to do something. It's strange to say, but I needed to lead him. I grabbed Urban by the arm and looked him in the eyes, saying, "Yo! Look at me! I didn't want those motherfuckers to score either, but if you can't score more than 7 points, then we don't deserve to be here anyways. Pick that shit up, and let's go win a football game!"

Coach Meyer appeared as though he had seen a ghost. He leaned over, picked up his headset, and directed the offense to take the field.

Although the game was momentarily competitive at 7-7, once our offense scored, that was it. Sure, it was tied, but when we realized we could score against them, our defense unleashed havoc. Our seven-man defensive front completely overwhelmed their offensive line.

I screamed out our defensive sets and glared at the offensive players with fury in my eyes. We terrorized Troy Smith, holding him to just four completions. Later, Troy Smith would admit that he thought I was utterly unhinged by the way I played that night. "I heard your voice constantly during every play. You never shut up. In my mind, when I think of Florida dudes, I still think of you that night." I was possessed, driven by a relentless pursuit of my vision. On one play, I blitzed and had a free shot at the quarterback. I had a choice: break down and secure the sack or try to take his head off. Naturally, I went for the latter, but he sidestepped me. Nevertheless, I forced him to his right and out of the pocket. My teammate Earl Everett pursued him, and an offensive lineman knocked off his helmet. What happened next became an iconic image in Florida Football history. Earl chased down Troy Smith and sacked him without his helmet. The sight of his dreadlocks waving in the air as he brought down the quarterback encapsulated the essence of that game. No matter what anyone did, we would not be denied.

We won the national championship game 41-14. When the confetti started falling, I couldn't hold back my emotions. That moment was indescribable. I was on top of the world, considering everything I had been through, from Pine Hills to Gainesville.

When you achieve something you desire, there is no feeling like it, but it also creates a longing for more. I wanted to feel that way all the time. I never wanted that high to fade.

Above all else, we had fun showing everyone who we were. It was the first game all season where everything clicked perfectly.

Before leaving campus for good, I took one of my teammates, Brandon Spikes, out onto the field. He was my successor and a linebacker with the same physical attributes and instinct for the ball that I had. In fact, Spikes would be even better than I was. I always believed he could go further and achieve more than anything I accomplished. I felt that way because I guided and taught him before it was his time to shine, and I always took pride in knowing I played a part in his growth.

I walked Spikes onto that empty field and said, "Look around. Do you see all this? I own it. This is mine. But now it's time for me to go. You know what that means. I'm passing it down to you. It's yours. Take care of it."

It was time for the next chapter of my life. I was heading to the NFL.

CHAPTER NINE

"NOBODY KNOWS WHO I AM"

Synopsis: As he transitions to being an NFL player, Brandon realizes that not everyone is on his side. Transitioning from notoriety to obscurity can be frustrating. Brandon shares his journey and how it changed his future.

During my mom's visit to the campus during my sophomore year of college, she reminded Coach Meyer of my vision for myself. I remember feeling a bit downcast as we met, as my mom explained the plan to him. "Now, Coach, you know that my son is going to the pros after this, right? You know he's only here for three years to win the national championship, and then it's off to the NFL." Urban looked at me and said, "Hey, if we win the national championship, he can do whatever he wants." Everyone was clear on my plan and my vision. I was so committed that I instructed my guidance counselors to set up my class schedule so I could graduate in three years.

I had fulfilled my part of the bargain, but I didn't expect him to fulfill his. After winning the national championship, emotions were high. Could we go back-to-back? Could we start a dynasty with Tim Tebow leading the offense? All these questions loomed in the conversations about our team, and I expected the coaching staff to try to convince me to come back and repeat our success. But no one ever did.

True greatness manifests when we encounter obstacles and surpass them. I believe that is why we face such trials.

No one asked me to return in the weeks and months after the championship, long after our celebrations and parties. No one sat down and made an attempt to convince me. Everyone just said cheerful goodbyes and wished me well. I was surprised but not offended at all. It was a testament to my reputation on campus and with my team. They couldn't imagine me going back on my word. Once I said something, I was committed to following through.

According to projections, I would be selected no later than the second round in the NFL Draft. My expectations were higher than that. My vision was that I would be the first linebacker taken off the board. Who could compete with my resume? I was the SEC Freshman

Player of the Year, a team captain, an SEC Champion, and a National Champion. On top of that, I maintained a 3.8 GPA. I was ready, but something made me doubt what I had already decided.

It could have been the fear of the unknown, uncertainty about what would happen next, or being overwhelmed by the responsibility. I remember sitting in my hotel room thinking, "Am I really about to do this?" Ultimately, I knew it was time for me to take this step. I needed my family to see me succeed, and I needed to get closer to the vision I saw when I closed my eyes.

If only I had known that I was in for a rude awakening.

Draft season is strange. Draft experts are not always former players or individuals who excelled in the sport. Many times they are analysts who religiously watch the game. They can analyze what happens on tape, but they've never witnessed the action in the trenches of the game.

Numerous sports writers have noted how strange the combine feels for Black players who are poked, prodded, and interrogated by mostly white executives looking for the right commodities to select for their teams. My combine experience was unsettling. For the first time on a football field, I felt like the people watching had no idea who I was.

One of the glamorous evaluations at the combine is the 40-yard dash. Scouts know the 40 times of players by heart and use it as one of the primary tools to evaluate high-value prospects. While I wasn't the world's greatest athlete, I was more than gifted and prepared for my evaluations. Every player gets two chances to run the 40 at the combine, in case one of their runs is a fluke or a mistake. As I stepped to the line, I knew I had to run well because my family was watching back home on ESPN. I ran twice in two different time slots and recorded a 4.59 both times. I knew I had made my family proud. There was only one problem: My runs weren't televised. Not only did they miss one of my runs, but they missed both by going to a commercial break on two different occasions. I was shocked. I was the captain of a national championship team. How did they not televise my runs? That felt strange to me.

The odd behavior continued when I sat with one of the Miami Dolphin executives. He asked me the standard interview questions, but as he asked them, he had a confused look on his face. He interrupted me mid-question, saying, "Hang on... Siler... Where do I know that name from? It sounds so familiar. Do you have any relatives in the league?" I said, "Uh, no, sir. My father tried out for San Francisco, but I don't have any other relatives. Well... my uncle did play in the league for a bit, but I don't really know him like tha--" he interrupted me again saying "Richard Siler. That's it."

I explained that I didn't have much of a relationship with my uncle at all, but the executive went off, ignoring my comment about my uncle. Apparently, my uncle had called him one day and acted like his agent to get signed to an NFL team. My uncle had fooled him into getting a roster spot, and the executive was embarrassed by the incident. I tried to reiterate again that I had nothing to do with my uncle, but the interview was ruined. He never let me tell my story.

At the end of the day, I had only received three visits from NFL teams. One of them was the Chargers, and during our conversation, they mentioned that they had a pick at the end of the first round. They were disappointed that they probably wouldn't get to select me. In their words, "We don't think you'll still be on the board by the time we get to pick."

The scarcity of visits was strange, but I was still confident that I would be a first-round pick. There was so much confidence in me that I debated whether I should run during my pro-day workouts at the University of Florida. These workouts are usually a showcase for athlete alumni to perform in front of select scouts. Because of our team's success, our pro day was packed.

Before the workouts, my agent advised me not to rerun the 40-yard dash. This went against my nature. I was a competitor and couldn't imagine sitting out when I had the chance to showcase my skills against others. They called my name, and I had a decision to make. "Maybe I should run..." Even Brandon Spikes was surprised, "You're not going to run? I thought you would want to show off your speed, bro." I decided not to run, and that turned out to be a mistake. My teammate Reggie Nelson ran a 4.39 during the pro day, compared to the 4.61 he ran at the combine.

Because of his quick time, he was selected in the first round of the draft.

I would have also significantly improved my 4.59 time. A team might have taken a chance on me in the first or second round. I may have had a longer career or a different situation. Maybe... but ultimately...

People didn't know who I was.

Draft Day was supposed to be the most fabulous day of my life. A boy from Pine Hills was supposed to walk into the NFL. I was prepared to receive the approval of my family and the players I already admired. I would prove to my family that I could make the vision come true, and my favorite players would now be my peers.

As the draft started, I had an eerie feeling about the day. I brushed it off as pre-draft jitters or imposter syndrome. My life was about to change. While I was confident in my abilities, the strange interviews and combine results brought me back to reality. I knew I wouldn't be a first-round pick, and when the Chargers made a late first-round selection of a wide receiver from LSU, I settled in for the next round. I was ready to hear my name, and after a few hours of listening to the commentators, I started feeling sick in the pit of my stomach. They didn't know who I was.

When I reached the end of the third round, I called my agent. "Did you put my name in? Did you do everything you were supposed to?" I didn't see my name on anything—no big board, no "top remaining players," not even anything for my position. I was devastated.

After the first day, I left my house, went to a hotel room, and cried. I was so disappointed. With every round I dropped, my chances of having a lucrative contract got smaller and smaller. When I emerged from the hotel and returned to the house on the second day of the draft, I asked my family where I had been drafted. I wanted to salvage some celebration for the people who loved me. The room fell silent. "What?" I said. "Was it the Raiders?" Everyone knew I didn't want to play for Oakland. "No... you haven't been drafted yet. It's the fifth round."

I remember legendary Hall of Fame linebacker, Ray Lewis, calling me that second day, filled with rage. "These motherfuckers don't know what they're doing! I can't believe this! Do they know how great you are?!" I appreciated Ray's encouragement, but all I could do was cry. "Man, don't worry about it, B. Just come over here. I'll tell them to sign you to the Ravens, and you can take this shit over. I'll pass the torch to you when I'm done, and you'll be the big dog after me!" I couldn't say anything to him. I was done.

The sixth round passed... then came the last round of the draft.

Right after Ray called me, Oakland called, saying they would select me. "Listen, don't waste your pick, Coach. I'm not playing football anymore. I'm done with this shit." I was truly done with all of it. Then, I got a call from Coach Ron Rivera.

If there's someone who has influenced me in the NFL, it's Coach Ron Rivera. At that time, he was the Linebacker Coach for the San Diego Chargers. Coach called me and was just as confused as I was about not being drafted yet, but he wasn't calling to encourage or console me. He was calling to draft me.

"Siler, you're going to be a Charger. We're going to draft you in the seventh round, you're going to be with me every day, and you're going to wear #59. You're going to prove everyone wrong and have a long career in the NFL."

59? That wasn't my number. Two years later, he told me why that number was significant. Coach Rivera wore #59 when he played. He said I would carry on his legacy in the league.

Coach Rivera is still one of the most beloved coaches I've ever had. He was more than a coach; he was a father figure to me. My two father figures were alive in reality but dead in my mind. When I was feeling low, he would comfort and encourage me with his words. When I was having a bad day, Ron would buy something for my son with a Gator on it and put it in my locker. Ron will always be someone I'm indebted to because he cared about my well-being. He is one of the most impactful people I've ever had in my life.

The draft experience was so painful that even to this day, it hurts to talk about it. Was there sabotage at play? Deep down in my heart, I genuinely believe I was sabotaged. It may not have been intentional malice, but there was a lack of enthusiasm about me. While we were successful and even won a national championship, Coach Charlie Strong and I never got along that well at Florida. As the defensive coordinator and team captain, that would normally be disastrous. Our coaching staff was so stacked then that it wasn't the end of the world.

Charlie and I had different processes for understanding our schemes. His process involved teaching the scheme and the technical side of the game with X's and O's. On the other hand, I wanted to know why we were doing it that way and how to execute it on the field. Coach Strong was not a natural teacher. I would always go to the Co-Defensive Coordinator, Coach Greg Madison, to understand the "why" behind the "what." To this day, Coach Strong and I still have no relationship, which leads me to believe he did not enthusiastically recommend me to the NFL coaches.

I was grateful to be in the league and fulfill this part of my vision. But this part of my life made no sense to me. For the first time in my life, I realized that there are uncontrollable variables. For years, my conviction was, "Do the work, and everything will work out just how you want it to." This entire experience shattered that theory in the most painful way. Here I was, a star athlete, an exemplary leader, an excellent student, and a national champion, yet I was only a seventh-round pick instead of a first-rounder.

My leadership skills expanded as I realized that not everything was under my control. My hard work and effort were only sometimes the ultimate measure of how far I could succeed in life. Life as a seventh-round draft pick was far different from anything else I had experienced. I was not the focus of the coaches' attention. They were concerned about their first or second-string players, their stars. I could barely get any reps on the field. I wasn't even on the scout team. The only time I could get on the field was during the special teams unit.

My face was on team posters, playing for a national championship, and I went from that, to being an afterthought. Eventually, I had to remind myself who I was and what I wanted to do. When I was younger, I fought for the starting spot, the advantageous position, the place where I felt I belonged. I had to return to my roots and ask myself the crucial question, "Who has what I want?"

I was grateful that San Diego drafted me, but I wasn't the only linebacker they selected. In the third round, they chose Clemson linebacker Anthony Waters. Anthony had talent, but it was insulting to be chosen after him, even with his injury history. Anthony hadn't played the entire senior year due to an injury. He wasn't active during the bowls or the national championship seasons. I firmly believed that Anthony Waters was not better than me.

As rookies, we all stayed in a hotel during training camp. We were required to have roommates. Training camp was highly restrictive. We had two-a-day practices, no freedom to roam, and everything was scheduled. This is why it's difficult for NFL players to transition into retirement. After that transition, no one tells you what to do, where to go, and when to do it. I was adjusting to the transition into the professional rhythm. It just so happened that my roommate was my fellow linebacker, Anthony Waters.

I would say to him, "You know I'm better than you, right?" Anthony would shake his head and chuckle. He needed to understand my determination and my passion to succeed. I started challenging him every day. "You owe me money, bro, so I'm going to beat you every day." "Man, Siler, you're crazy."

But I couldn't have been more serious.

I set that goal and put everything behind it. All my focus, consistency, hard work, dedication, and effort were dedicated to outperforming him right in front of me. The only way I knew how to do it, was to overdo it. Whenever they asked him a question in a meeting, I would answer it. When we were in line to eat, I would get mashed potatoes ahead of him. When we ran drills, I would never let him win anything. It was my sole focus every day in training camp. Anthony had what I wanted.

He has never beaten me in anything: no sprint, no workout, no drill. I resolved that I couldn't take back what had happened, but I damn sure could earn my respect from him and the team.

At first, people acted like they didn't notice. They didn't believe I could keep it up, but that's exactly what I did. Everyone else could feel my pain, and people understood what I was going through. They knew I had a vision for myself, and I felt like it was slipping away.

It's important to understand that the majority of preparation in the NFL happens in the classroom. When people talk about the speed of the game, they're not referring to physical speed. They're talking about the speed of strategy, preparation, and studying tendencies. Experience is the true measure of speed.

As rookies, we weren't aware of that, so our ideas of how much we should play were about more than just talent and athleticism. As rookies, both Anthony and I played on special teams. While we learned the details of the playbook, we had to sacrifice our bodies on kickoffs and punts. I was being treated like a seventh-rounder, and all I could do was resolve not to give up, no matter how difficult my situation became.

I worked with such intensity on special teams that the special teams coach spoke up on my behalf. "We need to acknowledge that Brandon outperforms Anthony every day. We all see this. He wins every drill and every workout. We see it on film every day. I know he's a third-rounder, but I need a real beast on special teams. Brandon excels on the special teams. So, give me Siler."

As we approached the preseason stretch, I was glad to have a role on the team, but I was devastated that it was limited to special teams. Special teams? Is that what it had come to? I couldn't see how this situation would bring me closer to my vision.

My situation went from bad to worse when I didn't even get to play in the first two preseason games. Would the coaches cut me from the team? Did I have a future in this league? I'll never forget going into that third preseason game. Our kicker launched the ball into the air, and tears filled my eyes on the field. I was failing, but I didn't want to give up. I put my head down and ran full speed at the returner. Like in my high school All-Star game, I exploded towards the returner, and he fumbled the ball. The team went wild, and I secured my spot on the special teams unit.

I should have been happy about this, but every win had its drawbacks. From then on, I was labeled a special teams player, not a linebacker. I couldn't receive a contract as a linebacker until I worked my way up the depth chart. All the practice reps I could get were gone. Every opportunity I was fighting for was slipping away. And frankly, I wanted to give up.

When I made the NFL roster, I was excited to finally play an NFL game. Even under the circumstances, something in me anticipated something great. The only problem was, I didn't know that I wouldn't be suiting up for that first game. Shockingly, I was unaware that a few players did not suit up for the team. I spent all night and all morning getting mentally prepared for this game, only to wear street clothes the whole time. It felt like a sick joke.

I was spiraling as I contemplated my life. I was a seventh-round pick, not a first-rounder. I was a special teams player, not a linebacker. I was a practice player, not a real professional. I was a failure. What good is a vision if it gives you false hope?

I returned to the same mental place after my father surprised me on that practice field. I lost the will to live.

I was driving my car near Lakeside, California, and the tears wouldn't stop. Who am I without football? What could I even do if I didn't wear this uniform? The thoughts overwhelmed me, and I decided I didn't want to feel that way anymore. I pulled my car over and drove off the ledge.

I attempted to commit suicide again, but this time, in a way that didn't give me a great chance of success. I thought this was the most efficient way to end my life, but I was sadly mistaken. I walked away from the accident almost unscathed, with minor scratches and bruises. I figured I was pretty lucky. I walked down the street to the Barona Casino and rented a room while waiting for someone to retrieve my car.

I sat on the edge of the bed and contemplated what had just happened. Right after I took that first deep breath, my phone rang. It was an old friend from Pine Hills named JR. He was involved in street life and lived the stereotypical life that ultimately cost him his own.

I assumed something was wrong, so I quickly answered the phone; his voice immediately cut through my "hello."

"B, God told me to call you. Are you alright?"
"Of course, I'm alright. You're tripping, bro." I couldn't tell him what had just happened. He would think I was crazy.

"Well, I'm not just calling you. I have something to tell you that God shared with me. God said that what you have now and what you will have in the future is right in front of you. He's going to show you that He is with you and will bring everything He promised into reality."

I wish someone could have taken a picture of my face. To my knowledge, JR was the opposite of a church person and had never set foot in a church. But he delivered God's message. Right in front of me, on the hotel room wall, there was an architectural sketch. It depicted the Barona Casino a hundred years earlier, and it was nothing more than a small hut. It was a hut, yet I was sitting in a room in this monumental casino. There was a web of interconnectedness and individuality that struck me. Was this what God was saying? Was He showing me that I was currently just a hut of what I would become someday? If so, I didn't want to see it.

JR and I spoke for an hour, and then we hung up. I stared at the picture on the wall and wondered what had just happened. I had an internal crisis on that bed. If there was a God, why would He want me to live? And if there was a God, how could He show me such a clear sign right after I tried to take my own life?

I was filled with disbelief and skepticism. I had no way of comprehending what had just occurred. My mind was a war zone, with rationality fighting against faith. The more I thought about it, the more I realized, I was meant to live. There had to be a reason I survived that accident.

The following day, I went back to practice with my team, pretending like nothing had happened. I continued playing on special teams, fighting for every opportunity to make a difference. Every time I stepped on the field, I gave it my all, knowing that it could be taken away from me at any moment.

As the season progressed, I finally got my shot at playing linebacker. Due to injuries and other circumstances, I was thrust into the starting lineup. I remember my first game against the Minnesota Vikings. My emotions were running high, and I was determined to make an impact. I recorded 10 tackles and made my presence felt on the field. That game served as a turning point in my career. I was no longer just a special teams player; I had proven that I could play linebacker at a high level.

From that moment on, I continued to work hard and improve. I became a key contributor on defense, earning the respect of my teammates and coaches. My perseverance paid off, and I solidified my place in the NFL.

Looking back, I realize that my journey was filled with setbacks, doubts, and moments of despair. It was also marked by resilience, determination, and the unwavering belief in my own abilities. I learned that success doesn't always come in the way we expect it to, and sometimes we have to redefine our goals and adapt to new circumstances. My vision may not have unfolded exactly as I had imagined, but I am proud of the journey and the person it has shaped me into.

Life is a series of challenges and opportunities, and it's up to us to make the most of them. We may face setbacks and obstacles along the way, but we should never let them define us. Instead, we should use them as fuel to drive us forward and prove to ourselves and others that we are capable of achieving greatness.

My NFL career had its ups and downs, but it also brought me incredible experiences, lifelong friendships, and the opportunity to make a difference on and off the field. Today, I look back on my time in the NFL with gratitude and appreciation for the lessons it taught me. It was a chapter of my life filled with growth, resilience, and the realization that sometimes the path to success is paved with unexpected challenges.

As I reflect on my journey, from a small neighborhood in Pine Hills to the NFL, I am grateful for every twist and turn, every setback and triumph. Each experience shaped me into the person I am today.

They taught me valuable lessons about perseverance, faith, and the power of believing in oneself.

To anyone facing their own challenges and pursuing their dreams, I would say this, never give up! Keep pushing forward, even when the odds seem stacked against you. Believe in yourself, trust in your abilities, and stay focused on your vision. Your journey may not unfold exactly as planned, but with determination and resilience, you can overcome any obstacle and achieve greatness. Keep the faith and never stop believing in the power of your dreams.

CHAPTER TEN

TWO STEPS
BACK

Synopsis: Why does success so often feel like you're taking two steps forward and five steps backward? Why does it feel like you've put in the work but cannot experience the benefits? Brandon wrestles with this reality as he continues his NFL career.

My first year in the league was challenging and a growing experience. While people often talk about achieving their dreams and reaching their desired level of experience, they rarely discuss what happens when you actually get there; it's not always what you expect. I'm not saying there weren't incredible moments in the NFL that changed my life, but it was different from what I had hoped.

Everything I had planned for myself was based on having a fair chance to play and demonstrate my value. In San Diego, I couldn't fully experience that. I began the year on special teams, channeling all my frustration into being the most disruptive tackler I could be. I wanted every team we played against to feel my impact and every coach on our team to recognize my contributions if given the opportunity.

Early on, I had hoped to get a chance to play on the renowned linebacker corps. Anthony Waters was injured for most of his first year, creating a gap in the depth chart. However, I was classified as a special teams player rather than a linebacker. I wondered if I would ever get the opportunity to prove myself on the defensive end.

After my first year in San Diego, I became one of the best special teams players in the league. I was known as a disrupter and a fierce competitor throughout the team, but they still relied on Anthony Waters to recover from his knee injury. Surprisingly, as the preseason of my second year approached, I still had the same uneasy feeling about making the team.

I was still trying to overcome the stigma of being viewed as a 7th-rounder rather than a 3rd-rounder. I was now labeled as a special teams player instead of a linebacker. Rarely did I line up with the defense in practice, so who would recognize my potential to lead the defense with intensity? Would I ever get that opportunity?

The feeling that kept resurfacing was the same one I had during the NFL Draft Combine: Did anyone know who I was? I felt overlooked and discouraged by the adversity I faced.

Fortunately, I made the team in my second year and excelled in any role they assigned me. I performed so well at my job that I led the entire NFL in special teams tackles. Now, I thought people would finally give me the respect and attention I deserved. However, even though I led the league in special teams tackles, my teammate Kassim Osgood was selected for the Pro Bowl instead of me. I was happy for him, but it was another example of being overlooked by those who could see my potential.

Adding to the equation, I was broke. Many assume that NFL players are rich and never have to worry about anything. In reality, my family and hometown depended on me, and I was still learning how to manage my money wisely. Our star linebacker, Shawn Merriman, was making $9 million per year, while Anthony Waters was making $2 million a year on his rookie contract. In contrast, I was earning the minimum salary, just $285,000 per year. Despite my meager salary compared to these players, I was still partying extravagantly and spending money as if I earned the same amount.

I can't deny it. We lived a wild lifestyle.

Merriman, Antonio Gates, Stephen Cooper, and I, along with others, had a ritual that we practiced as we lived out our wildest dreams in the NFL. A party bus would pick each of us up before the games. We would pack our bags for a two-day trip, and the bus would drop us off at the game while taking our bags to the private jet parked near the stadium. After the game, we would quickly shower and dress before our head coach, Norv Turner, delivered his post-game speech. Once the speech was over, we had a 10-minute cool-down period before the media entered the locker room. However, we were already dressed and would leave the locker room and board the jet within those 10 minutes. The private jet would take us to cities like Vegas, LA, Scottsdale, or wherever we chose. Sometimes, we would arrive in Vegas so quickly that we could watch our teammates' live post-game interviews in the locker room back in San Diego from inside the MGM. We would party as if there was no tomorrow. We were so wild that Stephen Cooper and Shawne Merriman once fought on the jet, with the rest of us trying to break them apart as the plane swerved back and forth, causing us to crash into the side of the aircraft. The pilot screamed over the intercom, "What are you all doing back there? We need to keep the weight balanced, or we'll crash." Yes, those were crazy times.

The NFL schedule was structured in a way that we played on Sundays, had full-day meetings on Mondays, and took Tuesdays off. Wednesdays marked the start of the work week for the upcoming game. We were so wild that when we won a game, we wouldn't even show up on Monday. We would skip the workday and coined the term "Victory Monday" to enjoy a long weekend, returning just in time for Wednesday's practice. Living in California was detrimental to my finances! I would go to clubs with the linebackers and my teammate, Marcus McNeal, spending thousands of dollars.

We always had the largest table, the wildest group, and the largest entourage at the club. It was a nightly occurrence. Initially, when I started playing in the league, I couldn't even get into clubs in LA. The bouncers would disrespect me and let others in but not me. Now? I practically owned the damn clubs. We were like rock stars in limos, private jets, and VIP sections. Eventually, I learned not to squander all my money, but at the time, I didn't care. I was living the life I had always desired.

During my third year, our team had several linebacker injuries, and I was no exception. I played the game with two torn groin muscles. It was incredibly painful, especially when sprinting 60 yards at top speed on special teams. However, I knew if I could play linebacker, I would still be healthy enough to excel. But when Stephen Cooper got hurt, they moved Tim Dobbins to my position because I still had the "Special Teamer" label with the coaching staff. We had a slow start that year, entering the game against the Kansas City Chiefs with a 2-3 record, while my injury became increasingly unbearable.

During the Kansas City game, the pain was so intense that I didn't think I could finish the game. After sprinting 60 yards to catch a returner, I went to the sidelines and told my Special Teams coach, Steve Crosby, "Hey Coach, I can't go anymore. I can't do it. I'm in too much pain." Right after making that admission, something unexpected happened.

Tim Dobbins, the guy in front of me on the depth chart, fell to the ground with a gruesome injury. I couldn't believe it. The moment I decided to step away, he got hurt. I looked at my coach with a slight grin and said, "Never mind, coach!" I grabbed my helmet and ran back onto the field, ready to prove my worth at last.

That's precisely what I did. At the end of the game, I was awarded the game ball for making the most significant impact. Despite having two torn groin muscles, I was named the most impactful player. That marked the start of one of the best streaks in my professional career. With me starting as the linebacker, our team won 10 straight games, and during that time, I received five game balls. I was flourishing, and the team was winning. This was my opportunity to secure a big contract and showcase my skills on defense.

Due to our success, we entered the playoffs and even had a bye week in the first round. During the bye week, the coaches instructed me to rest and focus on recovery in the training room to prepare for the playoff run. Finally, I felt the respect and appreciation I deserved. They valued me as their starting linebacker, resting me to ensure I was in top shape for the crucial playoff games. For the first time in my career, I felt content. It took ten wins to overcome the doubts of the other linebackers, who had all returned from their injuries, but I did it, and everyone acknowledged my talent and leadership. I finally had the recognition I deserved, even though it was short-lived.

After the fourth year, my contract with San Diego ended, and I wanted them to re-sign me as a starter on a favorable contract. However, Ron Rivera had left for the Chicago Bears as their head coach, and the remaining coaches still saw me as a special teams player. Consequently, I had to move on and find a team that would value my abilities.

Although I knew I wouldn't sign with San Diego, considering my performance, I believed I was about to secure a lucrative deal in the open market. My agent informed me that I should expect offers ranging from 3 to 5 million dollars per year. He said there were approximately four teams interested in me at that price range. However, things didn't go as planned. The following year, a lengthy lockout affected the league, drastically reducing the amount of money players could secure on the open market.

Once the lockout was lifted, free agency became chaotic. Players started signing low-value contracts out of fear that other free agents would be signed before them, potentially leaving them without a team. This drove contract values down significantly, affecting me negatively. Two teams that were considering me at the 3-5 million dollar range signed linebackers in my position for far less money. The best option I had was to sign a 1-year deal with the Chiefs for 1 million dollars, proving myself before securing a bigger payday the following year. The Chiefs wanted me as their starting linebacker, replacing Jevon Belcher. It felt different from San Diego, where I constantly had to prove myself. In Kansas City, I found security and confidence.

The Chiefs organization was first-class and did an excellent job of integrating me into the team. This was my breakout year. I was in great shape, happy, and eager to prove myself. I had spent the entire summer training in Miami and was in better shape than ever. When I arrived in Kansas City, I looked exceptional on the field, and my coaches and teammates appreciated my contributions. However, tragedy struck once again.

On the last practice play before our final preseason game, I lined up in our goal-line package opposite Thomas Jones (once again). I wanted to stop him from scoring a touchdown by meeting him in the air, but as soon as I jumped, I fell to the ground. Confused, I looked down at my legs. I had ruptured my Achilles tendon. I cried in agony as I watched my season disappear before it even started. I had been at my peak that offseason, forming a bond with Pro Bowl Linebacker, Derrick Johnson. We both knew it was going to be a great year for us. Yet, lying on the ground at the end of practice, I realized it was all gone.

Fortunately, my money was guaranteed, allowing me to financially survive that year as I recovered from my injury. However, the disappointment remained. To make matters worse, even after the season, I was still recovering. Although I was still under contract, I couldn't sign a new contract with the Chiefs before free agency because I had signed a minimum deal. That was an NFL rule. I couldn't understand why that rule existed and to whom it benefited, but that's what my agent told me. I realized that the Chiefs recognized my potential because they had witnessed my skills in practice before my injury. However, if I entered free agency while recovering from an

Achilles tear and riding a scooter, I would have little leverage in the market. I needed to take action; otherwise, I might not have a team to play for once I healed.

If you know me, you know I never take anyone's word for granted. I decided to research the league's regulations myself. During my investigation, I discovered a potential loophole in the NFL's policy. Even though I had signed a minimum deal, the team had given me a small signing bonus. In my opinion, receiving just a dollar more than the minimum shouldn't qualify as a minimum deal. I approached my general manager with this information, asking, "Didn't you guys give me a signing bonus?" The GM responded, "Yes, of course we did." I replied, "Well, wouldn't that make it more than a minimum deal because of the additional income?"

He paused. What he said next would determine my future and change my family's lives for generations. "Siler... you're absolutely right! Wow, that means we can probably sign you. You know what I'm going to do? I'm going to call the NFL office and see if you are right." If it turned out I was right, it meant that I had negotiated my own contract. This realization laid the foundation for my future career as an agent, eventually earning me millions of dollars after football. I took charge of my vision and refused to accept no for an answer.

For many of us, it's easy to rely on someone else's word and find ourselves in a less-than-ideal situation that doesn't create the best experience or the most lucrative outcome. I found myself in such a situation, torn between what I desired and what seemed possible. However, when you research things on your own and apply your knowledge and understanding, the possibilities become limitless. I had to take ownership of my vision before entrusting it to anyone else. I needed to double and triple-check what was possible.

I re-signed with the Chiefs and started playing for an organization I deeply respected. As I entered my sixth NFL season, I had high hopes that my life was finally stabilizing, allowing me to enjoy being a professional football player. We aimed to win a Super Bowl, and I aspired to make the Pro Bowl and secure a significant contract after the season. The sky was the limit.

Little did I know that this would be my final NFL season, not because I was forced out, but because I chose to leave.

Jovan Belcher was like a brother to me. We shared many similarities and enjoyed the same things. We laughed at the same jokes, shared common interests, and brought our families together for fun and fellowship. People wouldn't suspect it, but Jovan was one of the most generous men I had ever met. He gave selflessly, loved his family, and supported his friends. He would give you the shirt off his back. Jovan, Derrick, and I were like a tight-knit trio on that team. Our bond couldn't have been stronger.

However, Jovan was involved in an unstable relationship. His fiancé had recently given birth to their baby, and for reasons we didn't fully comprehend, they were experiencing issues related to the child. They were still living together until it became unbearable, leading her to move out of their house. To make matters worse, she was using the baby as leverage to emotionally hurt and manipulate him. One day, during a conversation about their situation, he casually mentioned, "I'll kill that b*tch about my baby, bruh." We immediately challenged him, saying, "No, bro, that's not true. Don't say that." But there was a look in his eyes that worried me. Jovan was a genuine person, and his expression reminded me of myself when I say something serious and everyone else assumes it's a joke.

My Saturday routine involved heading to the steam room, followed by a sauna session before the cold tub, preparing for the next day's game. On that particular Saturday, I overslept. I woke up when I received a call in the early morning hours. DJ sounded concerned on the other end, asking, "B, where are you?"

"Man, I skip the morning session for one day, and y'all boys can't ta-" But DJ interrupted me, "B, get down here. I saw Jovan walk by the locker room with a gun." My heart started racing. "He has a gun? What do you mean? Put him on the phone."

DJ's voice grew more frantic, "No, bro, they've locked us in the locker room. Hurry up and get here, bruh."

I leaped out of bed and rushed to my car. I sped away while continuously trying to call Jovan, but he didn't answer. Jovan had made the biggest mistake of his life; he had killed his child's mother.

Earlier that day, he had argued with her at their house regarding their child. In a fit of rage, he shot her to death. In his despair, he went to the only place where he thought he would be heard, the stadium. The blood stains on his shirt told the story. She was dead, and he had lost control. With a gun in his hand, he walked into the facility and requested that the head coach, defensive coordinator, and general manager come outside to talk to him.

I was speeding to get to my friend before he harmed himself or anyone else. The Chiefs organization is one that I will always support. In times of despair and sorrow, they have shown themselves to be a true family through their words and actions. On that day, the head coach, defensive coordinator, and general manager stepped outside the facility to meet Jovan and attempt to reason with him. I don't know of any other coaching staff that would have done that. Jovan stood a few feet away and calmly admitted, "I messed up and can't undo it. I fucked up, and there's nothing I can do to fix it. But before I leave this world, I wanted to thank y'all. Thank you for allowing me to play the game I loved and live out my dream."

As I approached the stadium, I kept trying to call Jovan, desperately hoping to convince him to stand down. The coaches pleaded with him to turn himself in and not take his own life. As I arrived in the parking lot, the police intercepted me. Just as Jovan was about to pull the trigger, the coaches asked about his daughter. Reality struck him. She was about to be left an orphan. He hesitated and said, "It's too late." All I heard was the sound of a gunshot echoing in the parking lot.

Jovan Belcher committed a heinous act, and our team was devastated. We mourned the loss of a brother, a sister, and an orphaned daughter who would have to grow up with the trauma of losing both her parents on the same day. The incident divided the team, creating a rift between those who recognized Jovan's goodness and those who believed his actions were too grave to find any good in him. I mourned my friend and his family. The problem was that we still had a football game to play the next day.

For years, I've tried to pinpoint the exact moment when I was done with football. As vividly as I can remember, it was that Sunday. Despite all the trauma that unfolded within the facility and outside the stadium, we still played football. I couldn't believe it. We had lost a friend in the most perplexing and violent way, and it didn't seem to matter to the league. It didn't even make national news. It was just a blip on the sports radar. What kind of game was this? The thirst for violence had drained from Jovan's last heartbeat. I was done.

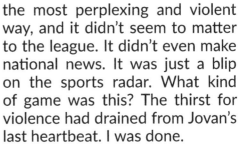

I took ownership of my vision and adamantly refused to accept "no" for an answer.

I finished the year, which was the last year of my contract with the Chiefs, and packed up my belongings. I regret not winning a Super Bowl. I regret not securing the big contract with the massive signing bonus. But ultimately, the NFL served its purpose for me. It wasn't where my journey ended; it was merely a stepping stone. I couldn't see it then, but what I would do after hanging up my jersey would impact more lives than I could ever imagine.

CHAPTER ELEVEN

THE TRANSITION

Synopsis: How do leaders pivot to greatness? In this chapter, Brandon details his transition to corporate America and the historic founding of Legacy Pro Sports.

I have yet to share one part of my vision. When I close my eyes and envision my future, my ten and twenty year plan doesn't involve a helmet or a football uniform. Instead, I see myself in a business suit, making deals.

After retiring from the NFL, I was uncertain about what would come next. It's not an ideal position to be an unemployed man with a family. However, one thing I did know was that I wanted to complete my degree at the University of Florida.

Seven years later, I returned to campus, committed to studying and completing my degree requirements. The only reason I didn't receive my degree earlier was due to my departure for the NFL combine. I was on track to finish my degree in three years and make a leap into the corporate world.

Brandon strategically navigated a series of transformative moves that propelled him into the next phase of his life...

Over the following years, I made strategic moves that propelled me into the next phase of my life and created a whole new experience. In this post-football phase, I've learned a valuable lesson. Every situation I've faced has contributed to my maturity and wisdom, enabling me to make the right decisions at the right time. This is a fundamental principle of leadership – when used to our advantage, nothing is wasted or lost. I have always had a knack for finding opportunities even in the most challenging circumstances, which led me to take risks and make life-changing decisions.

Upon graduating from Florida, I recognized the need to leverage my connections with the football team to enter the corporate world. Coaching wasn't my desired path; I understood the demanding nature of the job, which wouldn't allow me to prioritize my family. I sought something lucrative that also provided the flexibility to be present for my wife and kids.

I arranged a meeting with the University of Florida Booster Club, a group of alumni with multimillion-dollar organizations and valuable connections. Most athletes don't think about life after their sport; their focus remains on playing. However, I had moved on from football mentally before it was finished with me. This gave me a significant advantage when I met with this influential group.

To be honest, I was initially scared to take this step. I was afraid that my drive and love for football had disappeared. I had never experienced life without the engine of athletic performance. Who would I be without it? While my talent alone wasn't solely responsible for my success on the field, my boundless drive always pushed me forward. Losing that drive felt like losing a part of myself. Transitioning away from the field was surreal, as I was stepping into a new vision detached from the game.

I also worried that the funding necessary for success would be tied to football. Without the millions of dollars from salaries and signing bonuses, I feared losing the advantage provided by my time on the field.

During the meeting, I assessed the situation and understood the importance of exuding confidence without being cocky. I needed to make a clear request without appearing desperate, as desperation would convey fear and deter their decision. The Booster Club admired me as a football player, and I aimed to show them my strategic plan to add value to their companies.

After lightening the mood with jokes and stories, I expressed, "I'm done with football. My playing days are over. Coaches may call, and if the offer is right, I might consider coaching. However, I've always been an intelligent person, maintaining high GPAs throughout high school and college. I want to start a new career, a career, not just a job. I'm not interested in manual labor or menial tasks. But if you have a company that needs fresh insights and a new perspective from someone outside your industry at a management level, I'm your guy. Call me and send me offers."

I left the room, overwhelmed with offers and bids. Many offers revolved around medical sales, as they recognized my persuasive speaking skills. One sales executive particularly intrigued me – he had won a national championship in the 90s. During our conversation, he mentioned a friend's company that could offer me a position. Little did I know, David Nabavi, the person I was speaking to, managed Cemex, the largest cement company globally. This conversation turned into a job interview.

"You don't know anything about concrete or ready mix," he remarked, "but if you can talk and explain like that, I'll put you in the room with the executives. They will hire you without a doubt." David offered me a management position, overseeing 300 employees, providing a new truck, covering my phone bill and gas expenses, and giving me a company credit card. He wanted me to gain experience in all aspects of the business and help me excel within the company. I learned a great deal from David and appreciated his mentorship during my time at Cemex.

Shortly after, Coach Meyer called me, urging me to join his coaching staff. He wanted me to fly out to the coaches' clinic in Indianapolis and meet with him and other potential hires. I considered the opportunity, not wanting to close the door on a coach I had a great relationship with. I asked Urban if I could attend the clinic the day after, and he agreed.

Before meeting with Cemex executives, I knew I had to approach the interview with the same confidence as I did when speaking in front of the Gator Boosters. Despite having no experience in the field, I couldn't doubt my abilities. I needed to project confidence, drive, intelligence, and leadership skills that transcended the company's management level. Most people enter interviews focused on what they can say to impress and secure the job. However, I had a different mindset. I aimed for the decision-makers to conclude, "We must secure him immediately and avoid offering anything that would undermine his abilities, as he might leave for coaching."

For this plan to work, I had to create a situation that would showcase the challenges they would face. Although I wanted the job more than coaching, it was advantageous to keep that to myself. I also informed Nabavi about Urban's eagerness to fly me out and convince me to coach. I mentioned that Urban had discussed a starting salary of $150,000. Although I hadn't discussed money with Urban, I preferred jumping into the corporate world. I knew that Nabavi would share this information with the decision-makers during my interview. Nabavi understood the plan and agreed, recognizing the significance of informing them accordingly.

During my meeting with Cemex executives, I impressed them. The president of the Florida office said, "Listen, I don't know about the rest of you, but I'm 100% sold on him." I expressed my interest and eagerly awaited their offer as I rushed out the door to catch my plane to Indianapolis for the coach meeting with Coach Meyer.

A few days later, Nabavi called me to inform me that Cemex had offered exactly what I wanted. I chose Cemex and entered a whole new world. Although it was a management role, I couldn't manage a business I was unfamiliar with. Nabavi allowed me to gain experience in every area of the company. My task was to learn every facet of that specific part of the business and report back once I had done so. Coming from a sports background, where every move was directed, this was my first experience with leadership without micromanagement. Being given an objective and the freedom to figure it out made me feel empowered, like a boss. This strategy became instrumental in how I approached running my own companies today.

I began working at a block plant, learning everything possible. Once I felt confident, I contacted Nabavi to inquire about the next step. I transitioned to a ready-mix plant, following a similar learning process. I even spent time with the truck drivers to understand their operations. After that, I moved to accounting and dispatch. Having experienced each sector of the business, Cemex assigned me to the sales department, where I managed six ready-mix plants, 200 trucks, and 350 employees. I approached this responsibility with the same tenacity and leadership qualities that earned Tim Tebow's admiration when he joined the team.

They assigned me to the apartment complex division. At the time, Cemex was known for expensive specialty concrete, like the type used in Disney World. However, we had no presence in the low-quality concrete typically used in apartment complexes. Consequently, we only held 5% of the apartment business in Central Florida. I saw an opportunity and partnered with Dewitt Custom Concrete, a father-son duo running a significant commercial and residential company. We built a strong relationship, and I convinced them it was time to showcase Cemex as their top choice when serving clients. By delivering outstanding performance on the first job, we proved our worth to Dewitt and Cemex. From there, we expanded and secured more projects, transforming Cemex's position in the apartment business.

When I left Cemex 2 1/2 years later, we had captured 65% of the apartment complex market share in Florida. We purposely limited our expansion to avoid monopolizing the industry. It was a wildly successful endeavor. Towards the end of my tenure, my approach to work differed from others. I found a balance, playing the middle ground to perfection. Cemex taught me both the positives and negatives of the corporate world. I discovered that my ability to think outside the box set me apart from most individuals in that environment. Moreover, my time at Cemex helped me better understand myself and my strengths, which were consistent regardless of the field I was in. I possessed confidence, drive, intelligence, and leadership skills capable of transcending any company. This confidence propelled me to create a company that would change my life and the lives of thousands of former NFL players who struggled to transition into life after football.

Following my Cemex experience, I encountered several former players who faced difficulties securing disability benefits from the NFL. These players were injured and entitled to the benefits promised by the league. As I researched the issue further, I realized the system was rigged against us. There were two significant flaws: a lack of knowledge about disabilities and the intricacies necessary to obtain disability funds efficiently. Many players would try, fail, and give up. The tipping point came when I discovered that only 5% of eligible NFL players were receiving disability benefits, despite many being eligible. This infuriated me, and I knew something had to be done. I researched and developed a system to advocate for athletes, and that's when Legacy Pro Sports was born.

Now, with over five thousand athletes as clients, our success rate stands at 79%. I helped these athletes by applying corporate lessons I learned at Cemex and integrating them into every aspect of our organization. We use group texts and spreadsheets to communicate with staff members and organize workflow. Legacy Pro Sports continued to grow beyond our expectations. Our first potential investor, Steve Kuhn, couldn't invest due to a technicality. However, the following day, thirty millionaires reached out to us. It was an unexpected turn of events. When we sought clarification on how they found us, they simply stated that if Steve Kuhn was that close to investing, there must be something special here. We also received guidance from Scott Edmonds, former CEO of Chico's clothing store, and Greg Faulkner, a prominent trader at Raymond James. Their insights helped us overcome various challenges we encountered.

I've had the privilege of learning from celebrities like Ja Rule and David Ortiz, as well as executives from large corporations, investment bankers, and financial traders. I've gained knowledge from renowned artists and comedians.

One of the crucial lessons I learned is that when you have a vision and wholeheartedly support it, people will invest in you. I also realized the importance of having an open vision and setting ambitious goals. My desires have evolved from wanting a fancy car (which I obtained) to wanting a plane, a vision I never dreamt of in my earlier years. This continuous learning, growth, and adjustment of my vision have shown me that there's always more that God has in store for me. My connections and adaptability have revealed new desires beyond what I initially envisioned.

Football was merely a stepping stone for me. It provided valuable lessons that launched me into the next phase of my vision.

CHAPTER TWELVE

I AM MY OWN ROLE MODEL

Synopsis: Who inspires you? Who is your role model? These questions have devolved into cliche and lost their significance. In this chapter, Brandon offers a different perspective: his only role model is the future version of himself and the legacy he leaves for others.

I have achieved some extraordinary things in my life. I reached the top of the college football world, played professional football, built multi-million dollar companies, and met famous celebrities. However, nothing compares to the feeling of holding my newborn sons in my arms.

It is no secret that my relationships with my father and stepfather have been challenging. I have gone through phases of hating them passionately, trying to build a relationship with them, and everything in between. They, along with my grandad, were selfish men. When my wife, Pam, and I decided to have children, I knew that something had to change.

We both wanted boys to carry on the Siler name for generations to come, and God blessed us with two amazing sons. When I held them in my arms at their birth, I realized that they were the most important part of my vision.

Leaving a legacy is what life is all about. Many of us talk about enhancing our lives with experiences to create the reality we desire, but what good is that reality if it doesn't continue after we're gone? I didn't want to be like my father or grandfather. I wanted to invest in my children's future with my actions and words.

Running multiple organizations and attending various events is a gift, but despite my busy schedule, I refuse to do anything that would keep me away from my sons' practices, games, school plays, or important events. I prioritize being by their side. Once, I had an event with a DJ friend in Miami, but I also needed to coach my kids' football team on Saturdays. To show up for my sons and emphasize their importance, I flew back to Orlando immediately after the Miami event. I coached their game on Saturday, then returned to Miami for the second night of the charity event. I am committed to being devoted to my family because all the luxuries in the world mean nothing if I don't have time for them.

A few years ago, my father re-entered our lives. Despite forgiving him, I had to set boundaries for my own mental health. I wanted my sons to get to know him, but they were hurt when he repeatedly let them down. They expected him to have the same values as me because we looked alike. I had to step in and protect them.

When we watched the LeBron James documentary, my sons realized the impact of not having a father figure. They became angry at the injustice, but I instructed them not to hold grudges. I wanted them to adjust their expectations and protect their own futures. I believe they will become stronger and better than me because they can quickly make these adjustments.

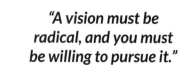

"A vision must be radical, and you must be willing to pursue it."

Parenting is a full-time job, and it's crucial to provide guidance, structure, and investment to our children. They need to understand our vision for their future and be immersed in family values. Parenting should not be treated as a part-time job. We must give our children far more than we had in our time.

Legacy is about how we impact the world while we're here and even after we're gone. That's why I have always incorporated legacy into my vision. It's not just about me; it's about positively impacting the world and leaving it better than I found it.

My best friend, James Thomas, also known as Jay or J-Baby, is one of the most influential people in my life. He is as much family to me, as anyone else. He provides me with truth, advice, and encouragement. When he needed financial help, I supported him because he had always been there for me. We worked together to achieve his coaching goals, and he ascended the coaching ranks at lightning speed.

In your circle, you need both the people who are always there for you and the ones who expand your vision. Surround yourself with those who challenge you and push you to take risks. These people will help you grow and achieve more.

As you develop your vision and leadership journey, remember this phrase: "I am my own role model." You don't need external motivation. Focus on developing yourself and your vision. Create an extreme vision that you can see yourself in. Break free from limitations, and evolve into everything you can be.

Vision goes beyond mere talk. It requires specific details and a willingness to pursue it relentlessly. **Close your eyes and envision your future, then open your eyes and go after it damn it!**

ADDITIONAL STORIES

Meeting President Obama

Here's something about me that you will soon learn by reading this book: I am incredibly resourceful. It would surprise you how resourceful I am when I desire to be in a room or experience something. During my NFL stint in Kansas City, I was recovering from an injury that sidelined me for the remainder of the season. While I was rehabbing, I received a message that motivated me.

After watching a TV report, my mom called me with exciting news. "Brandon, did you know that Barack Obama is coming to Orlando, and he's going to be at the Morgan's house?" I sat up quickly. "What did you just say? If he's going to be there, I am too." This moment presented an opportunity to bring two parts of my world together in an unlikely way. On one hand, the Morgans have a special place in my heart. They are known as powerful lawyers in the state of Florida and influential figures in the political world. After high school, before my transition to Gainesville, the Morgans were responsible for moving me out of the projects and moving me across town to live in a different place. Ironically, I lived in a place called GatorLand that is known for housing wild animals used at Disney theme parks. During that time, I gained 20 pounds from eating and working out, which prepared me to enter Florida in much better shape than I had been before. The Morgans represented a special place in my transition from high school to college.

On the other hand, everyone knows just how much Barack Obama means to the Black community. His smooth talk, calm personality, and loving family captivated all of us as we watched him rise to The White House, a place that was not designed for his presence. All the clichés like "You can be whatever you want to be" seemed more real after seeing him as our President. There was no way I could miss bringing these two worlds together.

I called Matt Morgan and said, "Hey man! I heard Obama is coming to your house! Yeah? Well, put me on the list. I'm on my way!" He was clearly startled by my determination. "Well... it doesn't really work like that. You have to get a background check with Secret Service and all that." I said, "Let's do it then because I'm on my way!" And of course, I booked the first flight to Orlando. Secret Service protection is not a game. To ensure the President's safety, they had helicopters flying around the house for three days before to monitor potential threats. In classic B. Siler fashion, I just walked right up to the front gate of the Morgan's house and stayed the night with them. I told Matt, "well if there are any problems, just tell them I'm one of the sons."

The next day, the President of the United States walked in. I had no idea what to expect, but I spent hours thinking about all the questions I wanted to ask him. I wanted to ask about his time in the White House, how he managed stress, what steps he took to walk into his place of purpose, etc. Surprisingly, I never got the chance to ask those questions. When I walked up to him, we took a picture together and he immediately said, "What's up, Brandon?" ...Wait, what? I was completely lost by the fact that he knew my name. I said, "You know my name?" He flashed that signature grin and said, "Of course, I was going to ask you: How does it feel to win a National Championship and make it to the NFL?" I stumbled through an answer, and he asked me two more questions. Before I knew it, he was gone. I was speechless.

Knowing that he was the leader of the free world, the President decided to take an interest in someone who was clearly excited to talk to him. That level of awareness blew me away and taught me a new level of leadership depth that shaped my future.

Mental Health Facility takeover

Another thing you will understand about me: I will always try to make sure that I look out for others, even when they are not looking out for themselves. A perfect example of this is in the Legacy Pro Sports business. Representing 4,500 athletes will cause you to realize that there are deeper issues at play than what you may have first thought. One of those major issues is found in athlete mental health. While we were helping one former NFL player, we sent him out to a facility so he could improve his mental health.

This rehab facility did tremendous work but was suffering from a lack of clientele. The athlete that I sent to the facility connected us in conversation. The woman who ran the clinic told us that she would give us a certain percentage of the profit if we kept the athletes flowing into the facility. After viewing the facility for myself, I saw how much she was struggling financially. We attempted to cut a deal with her and were constantly running into obstacles. Eventually, we even required a mediator to work through financial details.

After working through the details, we made an agreement that I would take over the company after a certain period of time. When she saw how profitable the business was becoming with our deal, she started to get cold feet about the transition. Every time I went back to her, there was some excuse. I realized that we would have to force her hand.

I decided to invest in getting a license to run a rehab facility. Through a consultant, I decided to invest part of the marketing funds we were receiving from the rehab facility into paying for the right to run the facility. After 6 months, we got everything taken care of and set. Now, we were licensed to run it in the state of Florida. All we needed was to find a building, which Pam was easily able to do. With the building under contract for 30 days, I came back to her and informed her that we had everything ready to break away from the deal that she set with me. I communicated with Maurice that I was no longer negotiating with her but would be willing to buy the facility under one condition: I must buy it within 30 days.

Essentially, I raised the stakes of the deal and put pressure on her to make a decision. I told her I would give her $2.5 million for the property with no questions asked. Before I went to her with the deal, I had attorneys prepare the contract and closed every door that could have been opened.

The most intriguing aspect of this deal is that I was able to buy this facility for almost nothing. I was connected with an SBA company that gave out millions of dollars of funding with a simple business plan and paperwork. After a lengthy process, we agreed to terms. Originally, I was going to pay the owner of the facility $1.2 million upfront and then $50,000 per month until she got paid off. The SBA company instead decided to loan me all the money that I needed to pay almost all the money upfront, with one stipulation. I wanted her to bonus me $280,000. Of course, she quickly agreed. I spent $20,000 of my own money and paid her with the same money that she had just sent me. When it was all said and done, I received $305,000 from the deal. What makes this even more unthinkable? The appraisal of the business came out to $17.5 million dollars.

What would have cost me millions actually gained me money and a $15 million valuation. Throughout all of this, I worked to get the best deal for myself, for her, and came out on top.

There is always a way to come out on top.

Celebrities

One of my core principles is: "No matter where I am, I will always be me." My good friend, DJ Irie, hosts an annual fundraiser in the Miami area with a massive celebrity presence. The event always showcases a "who's who" of famous faces. People like Alonzo Mourning, Gabrielle Union, Dwayne Wade, Jamie Foxx, and LeBron James are regulars at his events. He raises money for at-risk children and worthy causes. If you know me, you know I love that type of community impact. During my first few years, I attended as a celebrity. Afterward, I decided to start sponsoring the event as Legacy Pro Sports, rather than just attending. Our team set up a tent to raise awareness and funds.

At one of these events, I rode past a booth and spotted a Keurig stand. If you know my wife, you know she is in love with Keurig coffeemakers. I hopped out of the vehicle and struck up a conversation with a woman who was at the booth. Coincidentally, she turned out to be the Vice President of Keurig. We chatted, and it was clear that she was moved by my personality and energy. She gifted me a few Keurig coffeemakers and took down my address to "send us something special." When the package arrived, I initially thought it was just another coffeemaker, so I left it in the box.

After she called me, I finally opened it. Inside, there was a Gator-wrapped Keurig that she had customized for me and my wife. I was deeply touched, and we quickly became friends. Soon after, we attended a birthday party with Kevin Hart. I bought a front table at the event for my clients, and coincidentally, it was placed right next to Kevin's table. One of my players asked me about renting a boat for the party, and I had to stop him. "Look, we don't need to do that. We probably won't want to leave the party, so let's skip that." When we got to the party, we had a great time, enjoying drinks and connecting with everyone.

I was standing on the couch with a few of our partners, and suddenly, I saw a boat pulling up to the dock. As it approached, I thought, "Wow, that's a nice boat. I wonder who it belongs to." Out of the corner of my eye, I noticed one of our players nodding with a big grin. "That's YOUR boat. Everyone who's with Legacy Pro Sports, head to the boat!"

We made a lasting impression that day. There has always been something about me that catches the attention of celebrities. I believe it's because I refuse to diminish myself, regardless of the environment I'm in. I will always be me.

Milton Keynes UK
Ingram Content Group UK Ltd.
UKHW010938221123
433051UK00003B/218